You're Not Very Important

Twelve Steps Away From Self-Esteem and Toward a Better World

Douglas W. Texter

You're Not Very Important

Twelve Steps Away From Self-Esteem and Toward a Better World

Douglas W. Texter

ISBN 1-894953-20-7
CGP-4004

Published by Liaison Press
an imprint of Creative Guy Publishing
http://www.liaisonpress.com

Published in Canada

Cover photo by Luca a.k.a aculine

You're Not Very Important

Twelve Steps Away From Self-Esteem and Toward a Better World

Douglas W. Texter

Acknowledgements:

Nothing is ever accomplished in isolation. Thanks to the following: Pete Allen, Megan Bulloch, Nick Mamatas, and Robert Darden for their help and their support of my writing endeavors.

§

Dedication:

This book is dedicated to the memory and legacy of Joseph Heller, my strong poet.

§

Introduction: Self-Esteem, a Lurking Monster 11

Chapter 1: The Myth of Planning 15

Chapter 2: The Myth of Education 27

Chapter 3: The Myth of Work 41

Chapter 4: The Myth of Mythology 63

Chapter 5: The Myth of Self-Actualization 73

Chapter 6: The Myth of Creativity 89

Chapter 7: The Myth of Self-Denial 123

Chapter 8: The Myth of Diversity 147

Chapter 9: The Myth of Philosophy 167

Chapter 10: The Myth of Social Activism 187

Chapter 11: The Myth of Vision 203

Chapter 12: The Myth of Sisyphus 215

About the Author 221

"The class struggle, which is always present to a historian influenced by Marx, is a fight for the crude and material things without which no refined and spiritual things could exist. Nevertheless, it is not in the form of the spoils which fall to the victor that the latter make their presence felt in the class struggle. They manifest themselves in this struggle as courage, humor, cunning and fortitude. They have retroactive force and will constantly call in question every victory, past and present, of the rulers." –Walter Benjamin

"That's some catch, that catch-22." –Joseph Heller

Introduction

Self-Esteem: A Lurking Monster

This book will not change your life! Do you think that you're special? You aren't! Do you think that you have hidden potential? You don't! Do you think that you should chase after those dreams you've only half-articulated (and even then, just to your teddy bear, Mr. Snuggles)? You shouldn't!

I wrote this book for two reasons. First, I wanted to make a big wad of cash without having to think very hard. Second, I wanted to combat the notion that the world would be a better place if only people raised their levels of self-esteem and chased after their dreams. This is, of course, utter nonsense.

Most of our dreams aren't worth getting out of bed for, let alone chasing after. In fact, many of our goals, if realized, would truly louse things up. For example, take Dave, a quiet guy just getting by at a car dealership. Barely able to sell the minimum number of vehicles mandated by that jerk-off boss of his, Dave attends *The Formula*, a workshop teaching its attendees how to "get it." Upon graduation, *The Formula*'s students chant, "I can, I can, I can," while visualizing a buttercup-filled field in which Julie Andrews perpetually sings "Edelweiss." Because of his participation in *The Formula*, Dave finds within himself the strength to admit that he can become the best salesman of Lincoln Continentals in the United States.

And he does. In fact, people who can't possibly afford one, people who can't even drive, begin to buy Lincolns from Dave. He does so well that the national sales office plucks Dave from his former obscurity at J. D. Smith Ford and Lincoln in Ripley, New York, and makes him the director of the nationwide Lincoln sales campaign. Still riding the high of his newfound self-love, Dave does swimmingly. Soon, almost a hundred million Americans abandon their fuel-efficient small cars, bicycles, subways, and feet. They tool around in their huge Lincolns. Public transportation systems begin to fold. Highways have to be widened, and neighborhoods must be demolished in order to accommodate the incredible number of wide-bodied cars now on the roads.

Ford officials are orgasmic over the sales figures, and Dave decides to take his dream overseas. He meets with the Chinese Premier, who is so impressed by Dave's self-confidence and ability to sing "Edelweiss" that he immediately proclaims a One-Man/One-Lincoln Policy and establishes a five-year plan to produce domestically one billion Lincoln Continentals. The Chinese soon discover that they don't have enough gas to keep their Lincolns purring, and they decide to take military action; they drive across the former Soviet Union—in their Lincolns, of course—toward the Middle East. Realizing that a way of life is at stake here, the United States responds in kind. And the Lincoln Wars begin. Millions are killed; the economies of both countries collapse, and the world standard of living returns to that of Wales in about 1345.

Clearly, high self-esteem is very dangerous. Those who believe in themselves generally hurt the rest of us unsure souls pretty badly, especially when they have box cutters. Something must be done, or, to be more accurate, something must *not* be done, and right now!

How not to do it: The Categorical Imperative in the Circumlocution Office

What do Immanuel Kant and Charles Dickens have in common, besides being rather dead? They both articulated visions of a world in which very little got done. Kant's Categorical Imperative offers a four-pronged test of the morality of actions. It works in the following way: First, conceive of an action: "I can drink eight glasses of Scotch a day." Then, make that action an imperative: "I must drink eight glasses of Scotch a day." Next, generalize that imperative:

"Everyone must drink eight glasses of Scotch a day." Finally, conceive of a world in which the imperative is generalized, and consider whether you would want to live in such a world. If everyone, all four billion of us, drank eight glasses of Scotch a day, the world would be a rather strange place.

What most philosophers—those consummate con artists—haven't talked very much about is that not many actions pass Kant's test. And that's just the point! The less we do, the less we screw things up.

On the other side of Europe from Immanuel Kant, the British author Charles Dickens wrote a book called *Little Dorrit*. In this novel there exists an imaginary agency called the Circumlocution Office. The CO's chief function—in fact, its only function—is to show people how not to get things done. Individuals with wild dreams of new inventions come here and are immediately talked out of their plans. If only such a place had existed when the first strip malls were being built or when those eager beavers at Dupont, probably over a few beers, thought that napalm would be a nifty thing to have around.

Consider this book to be your own Circumlocution Office, a wise advisor whose only informing value comes straight from Immanuel Kant: *Do Nothing!*

Who the hell do you think you are: Bursting the Myths

In the chapters that follow, I will raze the foundations upon which the self-esteem movement that could destroy us is based. I will help you to tear down your self-esteem and save the rest of us from whatever really awful plans your ambitions may engender. But unlike other satirists, I won't just rip things apart. I'll give you concrete steps not to take.

§

Chapter 1:
The Myth of Planning

Let's begin at the beginning, a very good place to start. Five-year plans, battle plans, short-term plans, dinner plans, floor plans; everyone has plans. It's all just a matter of planning. Many self-help gurus rabidly discuss planning, and most advocate setting goals with the end in mind. The trouble is that these sages never bother to mention that most ends involved the exploitation of other people. The more ambitious the plan is, the more completely people are ground up by the scheme's cogs and wheels. Let's look at the First Law of Planning: For every step of the plan that you achieve, somebody else suffers. Since quite a few plans involve the transfer of money from one set of hands to another, it is well to remember the words of the French philosopher Montesquieu: "Property is theft." That's right; the money that goes into your pocket comes out of mine, and, when you buy this book, the reverse is, I am delighted to say, all too true.

In order to see the potentially disastrous consequences of goal setting, let's look at a specific example. There is a woman named Tiffany who is a sales representative for Plotnick's Textbook Publishing Company. You say, "Well, selling textbooks is a noble occupation, since it is intimately involved with the dissemination of knowledge." Although this, one could argue, is at least partially true, it's probably more accurate to say that it is intimately involved with the dissemination of napping. But no matter.

When she was twelve years old and her classmates at St. Raoul Elementary School spent their recess playing kick ball, Tiffany—to the consternation of the faculty—spent her free time reading *Unlimited Power* by Anthony Robbins and composing her long-range plan to retire to Monaco by the time she turned thirty-seven. She wanted to be able to make money and to take revenge upon her classmates, who always called her a nerd. So, while her young colleagues were thinking about kissing, Tiffany schemed of ways to eventually become the president of a textbook publishing company and to help bore the children of her classmates silly.

Tiffany is now twenty-six-years-old and on her way to achieving her long-range goal. Her short-term objective is to be the most successful textbook salesperson in the United States. She not only wants to beat the competition; she wants to drive it into the ground. Tiffany's defining paradigm is not *win/win.* It is not even *win/lose.* It is *win/eviscerate.* As we join Tiffany, she is about to make a presentation to the adoption committee from the English and Rhetoric Department of Jenkinville Community College in Boganville, Florida. Tiffany knows that one is more likely to achieve a specific goal if one has written down that goal and the steps necessary to achieve it. Therefore, she has composed a very specific action plan for securing the two-thousand-student adoption of an outrageously expensive business-writing textbook composed by Ralph Uppington. Ralph is a nebbishy little man with crossed eyes and a huge stock portfolio. He teaches at an obscure community college in Jersey City and thinks that Strunk and White refers to the name of a small-cap mutual fund. In order to secure the adoption, Tiffany has composed the following action plan:

- Lie about how good our book is.
- Lie about how bad their book is.
- Take adoption committee out for three-martini lunch.
- Leave lots of samples.
- Take adoption committee out for three-martini dinner.
- Cut brake cable of competing sales rep's car.

Tiffany's main rival from a competing publishing company is Fred Blivens—a man who can barely read and who also excels at selling English textbooks. Fred hasn't composed a plan for world domination; he merely wants to support his wife, who suffers from Attention Deficit Disorder, and his three young children—aged nine, twelve, and thirty-seven. He also is responsible for the care of his ninety-four-year-old mother, who is on a respirator at the Little Step-Sisters of Mercy Nursing Home.

Both Tiffany and Fred make their afternoon and evening presentations to Dr. John McQuincy and the rest of the Jenkinville adoption committee. Believing that he can win the day on the merits of his company's text, *Giving Them the Business: Corporate Writing for Fun and Profit*, Fred makes a fine presentation. But he doesn't understand why the committee seems to be staring at him with glassy eyes. Unbeknownst to Fred, Tiffany has been pouring alcohol down every throat that she can find, and her presentation is spectacular. She promises that her company's text, *To Market, To Market: The Really Ultimate Guide to Completely Stellar Business Writing*, will produce the next generation of corporate lackeys who possess prose styles rivaling that of Lewis Lapham, whoever he is. Reading from the selling script with which the advertising department has armed her, she claims that *Giving Them the Business* is an inferior text known to cause cancer in laboratory mice that eat it. The committee is stoked by the martinis and outraged by the heretofore unknown carcinogenic nature of *Giving Them the Business*. Dorothea Murphy, co-chair of the department, belches and asks rhetorically, "What if one of our students happens to eat a page on comma splices? Who's going to be held liable? Will your company pick up the tab for such a disaster, Fred?"

Tiffany chimes in helpfully: "Just a reminder, Dorothea, that if one of your students happens to eat some of *To Market, To Market*, he will find that a page provides a full day's supply of iron and Vitamins A, C, and D. In addition, one of our sister companies is developing a set of the collected works of George Orwell, a set that features an excursus on colon cancer. If you adopt our book, I'm sure that we can work out a shrink-wrap package. Your students will learn 'Politics and the English Language' as well as the basics of colonic health." Dorothea and the rest of the committee nod sagaciously.

Fred tries to deny the harmful nature of *Giving Them the Business*, but he realizes that he has probably lost the day. He promises to bring with him for the final presentation the following morning the nutritional descriptions of the titles on his company's back list. He has never had anything like this happen before and doesn't really know how to deal with it.

Fred and Tiffany leave the Jenkinville meeting to drive back to their hotels. The committee will deliberate this evening. At his hotel, which he barely reaches because of a mysterious problem with his car's brakes, Fred calls his regional sales manager, Chet Watkins. Fred asks Chet for some information on the nutritional value of the rest of the list. Chet has never heard of such a problem occurring with an adoption, and he yells at Fred for not having this information at his fingertips. "Don't you realize, Fred, that it is the duty of every sales representative of this company to completely know every facet of each book on the list? If you lose this adoption, Fred baby, your head is going to roll. Make something up. That always works. Now, get your ass in gear." Chet hangs up the phone.

Consumed by pictures of the nuns at the Little Step-Sisters of Mercy switching off his mother's ventilator due to lack of payment, Fred spends the rest of the evening trying to determine the caloric value of each page of *Giving Them the Business*.

Meanwhile, Tiffany is back at her own hotel, talking to her regional manager, Nick McGraw: "Nick, you'll never guess what I used. Yeah, that cancer-in-lab-mice stuff. Fred didn't know what hit him. I'm going to make bonus for sure on this gig. Just expect my T&E to be huge this month. I'm taking the entire committee out for a Bloody Mary breakfast in the morning before the final meeting." Nick compliments her on the fantastic job that she's been doing and wishes her all the best for the next day.

Tiffany says goodbye to Nick, and she checks off on her to-do list all the goals that she has accomplished. (For a complete picture of the damage caused by to-do lists, see *Table One*.) She watches Oprah for a while and muses quietly to herself about how nice it would be to have a talk show of her own. Then she switches the set off in order to practice the technique of creative visualization that she learned from reading *Ninety-Seven Habits of Really Rapacious People*. She has done this every evening of her incredibly successful sales career, and the results, as we can see, have been staggering.

In her visualization, she creates a mental picture of the result that she wants to have happen. For this particular scene, she creates an image of herself atop a jewel-encrusted elephant that has one foot planted firmly on the chest of Fred Blivens. Each element in the scene symbolizes a step of her final plan. The elephant stands for the adoption. The jewels represent her bonus for securing the adoption. And Fred...well, Fred is Fred. She has fed and watered the elephant. And she plans to give it one final meal in the morning before the adoption-committee meeting. Her visualization complete, and victory nearly assured, Tiffany goes to sleep and dreams of Robin Leach conducting a tour through her new home-of-the-stars in Monaco.

The next morning goes wonderfully for Tiffany. The adoption committee sways from the Bloody Marys that Tiffany has provided. And it will not be convinced by Fred's rather bleating argument that *Giving Them the Business* is not carcinogenic and is in fact as tasty and nutritious as *To Market, To Market*. Jenkinville decides to adopt the book from Tiffany's company.

True to Tiffany's vision, the elephant dances on Fred's chest. Tiffany receives a twenty thousand dollar bonus for securing the adoption, and within six months she is promoted to national sales manager. Three years later, she becomes the president of the company and builds her dream home in Monaco. Fred, though, does not fare so well. He is fired from his job. And his mother's respirator is in fact turned off by the Little Step-Sisters of Mercy. The nuns believe in compassion, but they also realize that a buck is a buck. After losing the mortgage on his home, Fred also loses his ADD-suffering wife. She conveniently forgets that she is married to him but remembers to have an affair with her therapist. She divorces Fred, who ends up as an alcoholic living in a YMCA while telemarketing for a credit-card company.

Table One: Why To-Do Lists are Harmful: Historical Data

Daily "To-Do" List Writer with High Self-Esteem	Items on Sample Daily To-Do List	Results of Accomplishment of Tasks
Pope Innocent III	**May 3, 1215**:	
	1. Crush all who resist Big Daddy's authority.	1. The Inquisition convened—thousands killed, tortured over 600 years.
	2. Launder cassock.	2. Really expensive purple robe ripped by Papal Launderer with hangover.
	3. Bail Jerusalem out of trouble again.	3. The Crusades continued; middle east turned into bloody mess for 800 years; hundreds of thousands killed, raped, plundered; World Trade Center destroyed by descendants of Crusade victims.
Robert Oppenheimer	**July 1, 1945**	
	1. Get new sunglasses.	1. Chuck Yeager laughs at Oppenheimer for thinking that physicists can be as hip as test pilots.
	2. See if my little physics experiment works.	2. World's first nuclear weapon detonated over New Mexico.
	3. Tell people about it if it does.	3. Hiroshima and Nagasaki turned into smoking ash piles; world at edge of nuclear destruction for next 45 years
Christopher Columbus	**November 3, 1492**	
	1. Go say hi to that nice short guy we saw on the beach.	1. Native Americans first exposed to European diseases; 20 million killed.
	2. Remember to plant flag Ferd gave me.	2. Colonial empires founded in New World; centuries-old civilizations wiped out.
	3. Ask short guy if he wants to go for ride in boat.	3. Slave trade started in North America; millions lose their freedom over next 350 years.
Saddam Hussein	**July 3, 1990**	
	1. Practice assertiveness-training techniques with U.S. Ambassador April Gillespe.	1. Kuwait invaded; Operation Desert Storm launched to give Kuwaitis back their own dictators; aging Red Adair gets to be in limelight for first time since John Wayne played him.
	2. Buy new, sportier beret.	2. Store out of berets; all haberdashers in nation immediately flogged.
	3. Get mustache trimmed.	3. Nicked by barber; barber's family summarily gassed; barbershop shelled.
Andrew Carnegie	**May 1, 1892**	
	1. Talk reasonably to the boys in the factories about personal responsibility.	1. Many workers shot by Pinkertons.
	2. Economize.	2. Surviving workers receive pay cuts.
	3. Take some time to do something for me.	3. Surviving workers shot

There it is, then, the difference between those who plan and those who don't. There are steps that you can take to ensure that the rest of us aren't destroyed by your machinations.

What not to do:

We can't undo the damage that Tiffany has created, but we can take some steps to ensure that we don't reach our goals and make things more screwed-up than they already are.

1. Don't write things down.

Goal-setting experts tell us that we are much more likely to do something if we have committed the particular objective to writing. Therefore, please, for God's sake, don't write your idea down. Or, if you feel that you simply must put the particular idea in writing, write it in your journal, and then make sure that you tear out the page and throw it away immediately. Thus, you will have no written record of your plan, dream, or ambition. And you will be much less likely to achieve it and much less likely to screw things up for the rest of us.

2. Don't keep track of your time.

Efficiency experts point out that time is the one commodity that you can't get more of. And thank god that's true. Most people don't keep very good track of their time, and, therefore, they aren't able to realize their goals. Fortunately, time just slips away. Don't you wish Hitler had been a time waster? Well, he wasn't. He kept a little Daytimer, the pages of which were calibrated in fifteen-minute segments. He made sure that every fifteen minutes he accomplished a new task, sometimes two. In order to see what a good user of time he was, let's look at a typical hour in the life of one of the biggest maniacs of the twentieth century: eight to nine o'clock on the morning of Thursday, May 16, 1940.

8:00-8:15: Floss teeth.
8:15-8:30: Revise plan for 1000-year Reich.
8:30-8:45: Discuss bombing campaign against England with Goering; don't forget to compliment the Air Minister on his choice of eyeliner today.
8:45-9:00: Pay electric bill for Berchesgarten.

So, don't keep track of time. You won't accomplish much. But you won't hurt anyone either.

3. Don't try to complete 'just one more task.'

Often it's that very last thing that we get done, that extra-special project that we stay late for, that extra mile that we walk that gets us into real trouble or causes harm to somebody else. Never, ever stay late, especially when you're not getting paid overtime for it. If you do stay, you might just get something done. And who knows how many people that new deal you've just finalized will put out of work. If you had delayed just one more day, maybe it would have fallen through and those people would still have jobs and a way to feed their families. But now, we'll never know. They're starving to death out on the street. Feel terrible? Good, you should.

§

Chapter 2:
The Myth of Education

From preschool to postdoctoral fellowships, Americans are preoccupied with getting an education. We are told by those supposedly in the know that if we just had more learning we would become richer, while the world would paradoxically become better. Thus, we scramble to go to school, to get back into school, or, in certain Midwestern states, to flee in terror from school. Education, say gurus such as Paolo Friere, can help to produce democratic, self-secure, and generally kind people. But is this really true? For example, what do Robert E. Lee, Ted Bundy, and Henry Kissinger have in common? They all went to school. And they all caused quite a bit of havoc afterwards. Consider: Robert E. Lee, a man who read the *Phaedrus* and defended slavery. Ted Bundy, a law student by day and serial killer in the evening. And Henry Kissinger, a general pain in the butt to denizens of both Harvard and Hanoi.

For a more immediate example, consider your next-door neighbor. He has just spent a year in his cubicle creating a marketing plan for the new hit CBS situation comedy, "Three Androgynous Men and a Baby of Rather Questionable Gender." More effective than even Stephen Covey and possessed of at least six and a half of the seven multiple intelligences plugged by Howard Gardener, this man is ultimately responsible for more mental death than even Samuel Beckett could have dreamt of.

Yet, this person—let's call him "Ben"—along with some of the brightest people in our nation, individuals who have spent years climbing Ivy-encrusted towers—is a prime example of what the supposedly best part of our educational system produces. Ben plans methodically, studies maniacally, and creates magnificently. All that labor gives him the bucks to travel to Maui several times a year with his older brother,

Zack, a self-help guru. But it produces a final work that is at best useless and at worst destructive. Where did Ben learn to work so hard and with such zeal for something he really doesn't care about? Why, in school, of course. Let's take a detailed look at this other peculiar institution and understand exactly how it works:

School days, school days, good old golden rule days. How many of us wax nostalgic about those orange and brown October afternoons, when the air was crisp and the sky a cobalt blue? Ah, those days of cheerleaders, football games, and Miss Higgenbottom's English class, in which we learned to write really bad haikus. As a certain hirsute singer from New Jersey rasps, these were the glory days.

Bullshit! School sucks, not only because it's full of icky people, many of whom perpetually smell like salami, but also because it's where we begin to plan our futures. The location from which we begin huffing and puffing down the wrong track toward a cubicle, school promises us culture, sophistication, and self-actualization. What does it deliver? Iggy. At fourteen—the average age of most members of the Hitler Youth—Iggy sports a shaved head and a nose ring. He weighs two hundred pounds, enjoys sitting on people as his sole form of recreation, and possesses a four-color chest-tattoo of Jesse the Body Ventura. He especially enjoys sitting on honor students with glasses, girls with large breasts, and anyone with zits. (See *Table Two*.) Iggy is suspected of having committed felonies in three midwestern states, which wish their names to be withheld.

Table Two: Two Hierarchies of Needs: Abraham Maslow vs. Iggy

Abraham Maslow	**Iggy**
Self-Actualization	Beer
Esteem	Sitting on Cute Girls with Big Breasts
Love	Beating up Nerds
Safety	Giving People The Atomic Elbow
Physiological	Beer

When most of us talk about our own time in school, we conveniently omit all reference to Iggy. Why? Because we must. Our very way of life depends on denying the existence of Iggy and his terrifying ilk. If any self-respecting and reasonably bright four-year-old—armed only with his Kermit the Frog lunch box—were apprised by his parents of Iggy's presence at the local school, he would immediately run away from home. In fact, he would probably flee the country, spitting on John Dewey's grave just before boarding the first flight to the Chilean Andes and his future vocation of llama herder. But Iggy is not the only terror awaiting the students of yesterday, today, and tomorrow. If the young scholar of our example—let's call him "Winston"—survives being used as Iggy's seat cushion, he's in for an even more rude awakening at the hands of his instructors.

Let's visit Winston when he is fourteen-years-old and attending his first high-school physical education class, which resembles a bad morning at Stalag Seventeen. Winston's class at St. Raoul Prep is conducted by Mr. Xerxes, who is also the school's athletic director and football coach. With straight, grey hair cut in Beatle-like fashion, Mr. Xerxes possesses a pockmarked face, the type of visage often seen in smoky bars in New Castle County, Maine. And a beer belly protrudes from beneath his optimistically tailored baby-blue Oxford shirt. In a coffee-cup strewn office in the school's athletic wing, Xerxes droolfully reminisces about the quarterback blitz for which he won the 1972 All-City football trophy. This monument to brute force sits on a table like a blood-bloated spider.

With the aid of his teammate Bill Zambini, Xerxes crippled Fred Smithers, the handsome young quarterback from East High. Before his encounter with Xerxes and Zambini, Smithers was speeding toward an incredible yards-gained record. Ah, Xerxes recalls so well that cold October night. The stadium was redolent with the aroma of mustard-slathered hotdogs and popcorn drenched in butter. He remembers the quart of Schlitz that he and Zambini shared in the locker-room during half-time and the steam rising from the bells of the marching band's brass line.

What Xerxes remembers most about that night, though, is the snap that emerged from deep inside the body of Fred Smithers, when he and Zambini caught the handsome young athlete like a rabbit crushed by a steel trap. "Fucking pretty boy ain't going to get his scholarship; we'll make fucking sure of that," he had—with a boozy breath—rasped to Zambini during half-time. Just as Smithers was about to receive a pass, Xerxes hit him from the front at chest level, and Zambini nailed Smithers from the back, almost exactly at the knees. Needless to say, Smithers never went to Notre Dame on that full scholarship. The Fighting Irish had no use for a quarterback needing to be wheeled onto the field.

After his football career crashed to a halt, Smithers still attended college, matriculating at St. Bartholomew's and majoring in English. He now teaches at Holy Conception University. What always struck Zambini as odd is that despite not being able to walk, Smithers did okay in life. He even spent a summer wheeling himself across the country. The local newspaper had cited Smithers' odyssey as "a prime example of human perseverance overcoming seemingly insurmountable obstacles." Zambini was much less complimentary of Smithers' triumph: "Prick."

In spite of Smithers' successful coping with his injury, Xerxes wouldn't trade that night in '71 for anything in the world. He had been able to hurt someone, really badly. And the opportunity had been given to him within the delightful parameters of a football game. That very audible snap of Fred Smithers' spine had been music to Xerxes' ears. In fact, when Xerxes tackled someone, he always sang "Louie Louie" to himself. He and Zambini hit Smithers on the beat at which "Ay" occurred. The only other time in Xerxes' life that he had experienced such joy was when, with cockroaches the size of gerbils in his foxhole, he listened to the screams of three Viet Cong guerillas after he had tossed a fragmentation grenade into their hooch. "God, life is great," Xerxes had thought after the explosion. "To be able to kill people and get paid for it."

It is into the keeping of this monstrosity and others equally reprehensible that Winston's parents, with the full sanction of the state, deliver their skinny and pubic-hair developing third-born for fifty minutes three times a week. Gym class for Winston and many of his non-athletic classmates represents the nadir of their existence.

With a shrill blast on his whistle, Xerxes welcomes Winston and his fellow inmates to the gymnasium, which reeks of floor wax and sweat: "Move it, ladies. Move it! I want you pansies on the line in three minutes. If you're late, you'll do laps until Hell freezes over. Move it! Move it!" Winston races down the stairs to the changing room and deposits in his locker his Algebra II book—in which one of his classmates has rendered gynecologically correct depictions of women's anatomy. Then he takes off his clothes and changes into his prescribed uniform, which consists of regulation sneakers, black running shorts, and a white t-shirt. This last item is emblazoned with a picture of the school's mascot, a large ram, in the process of butting some unseen adversary. From the top of the stairs, Xerxes gently reminds his charges of the time constraints under which they labor: "Move it. One minute and fifty seconds. You guys'll run laps all period. I'll burn that disgusting baby fat off you sissies! You're going to hurt for days. Move it! Move it!"

Winston runs upstairs and arrives at his alphabetically assigned spot on the black line. Carrying a clipboard with a copy of the class roster, Xerxes mimics the warden in *Cool Hand Luke*. He walks slowly from one end of the line to the other. As he stops in front of each student, he looks directly into the kid's eyes, as if trying to peer into the student's depraved soul. Xerxes occasionally orders one of his charges to tuck in his shirt or to stand up straight. The gym instructor firmly believes that by subjecting his students to harsh discipline early in life, he can instill in them pride, something that they will thank him for later when they have become successful criminal-defense attorneys and, in some cases, successful criminals. Many of Xerxes's students will always remember him fondly as a mentor; they will remain faithful to him in the same way in which a kicked dog will remain loyal to the owner of the offending foot.

Arriving at Winston's place in the line and spotting the bottom of our young hero's shirt rebelliously peeking out over his running shorts, Xerxes, playing Socrates, stops and poses two rhetorical questions: "What do we have here? Didn't I just tell you to tuck that in?"

Winston is completely out of breath and a little stunned from trying to memorize irregular forms of "-er" stem-change verbs for his Spanish quiz next period. He stammers: "I'm sorry."

Xerxes is not satisfied with Winston's verbally expressed remorse. The coach demands a physical act of contrition: "Well, you won't forget when I'm done with you. Run two laps now. That'll teach you to be neat." On Xerxes's shirt are several coffee stains. A drinker of about eight cups of Ishmael's Caffeine Machine coffee a day, the gym instructor continues: "It'll help you to lose those fat legs of yours. You look like a girl."

Freeze frame! Winston has just received his first lesson in humiliation, the most important subject taught in our nation's schools. The rather naughty theorist Michel Foucault astutely noted that our motherland's educational facilities greatly resemble our prisons, which, in turn, look strikingly similar to our offices. Have you served time in a cubicle lately? If everybody were confident about their abilities and appearance, how could the purveyors of the self-esteem flogged on late-night television and hawked by early-millennium capitalism exploit them fully? Imagine an office crammed with people who really know what they want! The place would be chaos in twenty minutes, with open warfare erupting around the copier and the coffee machine. Humiliation prevents people from stepping out of their assigned slots, and the hiring of someone smarter than you really exists as a fine way of keeping the competition under control.

Duly embarrassed, Winston runs his two laps and then returns to his place in the line. He is appropriately cowering in front of his sniggering classmates. With a vindictive twinkle in his eye, Xerxes instructs his students to count off in twos. One-two, one-two, one-two. Ones are skins, and twos are shirts. The skins peel off the tops of their uniforms and deposit them on the polished wooden bleachers. Anticipating with relish the creation of an atmosphere of unmitigated mayhem, Xerxes brings out a white cotton bag. From inside the sack bulge—like unwanted kittens doomed to be cast off a bridge—twelve pinkish rubber balls, each about the size of a typical human head. Xerxes announces to the students, who still toe the line, that they will while away the next forty minutes or so playing dodgeball.

Dodgeball is the perfect manifestation of cruelty masquerading as athletics. If you play dodgeball, you possess only two goals: first, to hurt your opponent, and second, to avoid his attempts to hurt you. In this fascinating game, the person who holds a ball selects a target from the ranks of students occupying the other side of the floor and fires the ball as hard as he can at the target. The person at whom the ball is aimed attempts to dodge the shot, hence the game's name. Victory is achieved when all the members of one team have been hit.

Winston possesses very weak reflexes but a very strong desire not to have his glasses sent flying across the room after a good head shot. Thus, he decides to commit hari-kari at the first possible opportunity, and he duly steps in front of the most sluggishly moving ball that he can find. Xerxes sees one of his students brilliantly execute what military theorists would call a strategic withdrawal. And he responds appropriately: "Hey, you little wuss."

Dodgeball, argue its proponents, supplies the incredible amount of physical activity afforded by standing stationary and then ducking very quickly. It also teaches invaluable skills and values. Like life itself—and especially life as spent by most people in large institutions such as the military, schools, and corporations—a dodgeball game generally consists of large periods of overwhelming boredom, punctuated by intense bursts of terror. Moreover, dodgeball prepares people for a life spent working in the employ of others by demonstrating with a clear simplicity found in almost no other sporting event that professional success consists largely of trying to eliminate one's opponents and avoiding their reciprocally directed machinations.

His skin red from the smack of the ball against his flesh, Winston sits out the rest of the game in the relative safety of the bleachers. And he vows to ask his parents to procure a doctor's excuse delivering him from the clutches of Xerxes. After the conclusion of the game, Winston descends once more to the locker room in order to shower and prepare for his next class.

Showering after gym is one of the truly traumatic events of puberty. One must strip naked in front of one's peers, who, at the age of fourteen, are none too accepting of any divergent body type. On this particular day, Winston becomes especially unlucky and is chosen by Frank Kelvington, a budding star of the freshman class and a future gas-station attendant, as the recipient of what is called in the vernacular of high-school a wedgie.

The process of giving a wedgie is strikingly similar in form to ancient Incan rituals of human sacrifice. Never before chronicled in print, the process is as follows: Wedgie participants, sporting glassy-eyed grins, circle the intended victim, grab the top strip of his underwear, and pull sharply upward. The wedgie is considered to have been successfully executed if the underwear becomes lodged in the victim's butt crack. It is even more successful if the top strip of the underwear tears during the struggle. It is wildly successful if the said undergarment tears off completely. If this last scenario is the case, an exuberant celebration ensues in which the wedgie participants dance in a circle around the now-groaning recipient and throw the torn undergarment onto the closest light fixture.

Winston will receive several wedgies and will therefore adopt the habit of carrying with him at all times a spare change of underwear.

Even when a wedgie is not part of the process, showering after gym class can be very bleak. Boys tend to talk about their schlongs and to compare them with those of their peers. One of Winston's friends, Jason Blackwell, asserts that Winston's penis is the smallest one he has ever seen, which indicates, of course, that Winston is a fag. New to the traditions and language of the locker room, Winston doesn't know exactly what a fag is. All that he is certain of is that being a fag entails the wearing of pink button-down shirts and the possession of an excessive fondness for *The Wizard of Oz*. But upon Jason's suggestion, Winston immediately, and for the next four years, until he clumsily copulates with Katie Simone on Prom Night, becomes deathly afraid that he is a fag.

Thus is one manifestation of school: a never-ending cycle

of boredom, terror, and needless humiliation. Somehow—and perhaps precisely because of its ridiculous nature—school works. There are, of course, exceptions. For example, there exist the educational institutions run for the unfortunates occupying inner-city slag heaps, such as North Philadelphia. The people in these institutions, possessed of the temerity to be poor in a nation in which not being rich—let alone being poor—is tantamount to criminality—these people simply do not count. So, let's leave them to their quite uninteresting and rather tacky fates. The case of the poverty-stricken notwithstanding, school works only too well. People depart from school and college and enter the intellectual charnel house of the marketplace, becoming successful salespersons of Lincoln Continentals and denizens of Cape Cod communities, such as the probably only too appropriately named Billingsgate.

Since the brightest students—such as Winston—are generally the ones treated most abominably by both instructors and fellow pupils, they're generally also the ones driven hardest to succeed in life. After all, success is the best revenge. In the back of every precocious pupil's mind, there exists a certain hope or expectation that Iggy, although now terrifying, will eventually wind up creating Slush Puppies at the local Seven/Eleven. It's at least partly as a reaction against the loathsome and pernicious influences of Iggy and Xerxes that young over-achievers are produced.

What Not To Do:

1. Parents: Don't send your children to school.

Withdraw your children from school immediately. Do your children know how to read, write, and perform simple mathematical operations? If they do, then they're already ahead of the graduates of most high schools and, unfortunately, some colleges. Thus, there doesn't really exist a very good reason for their attendance in the academy. In addition, the longer you keep your children out of the embrace of Xerxes, the more unlikely it will be that they will want to do well in school, go to a good college or university, and then double major in accounting and gerontology. Their ultimate aim will be to put old codgers in retirement communities that feature shuffleboard for recreation and cream of wheat for breakfast, lunch, and dinner. Remember, it's in your own best interest to keep your children out of school. The school child of today could very well become the corporate drone of tomorrow. With his DayTimer in one hand and his to-do list in the other, he'll create the next generation of thermonuclear warheads.

2. Kids: Don't go to school.

Learn how to read, write, and calculate. You don't need to be hooked on phonics in order to master any of these tasks. And once you've learned to perform these operations, get out of school as quickly as you can. The longer you stay, the more likely it becomes that you—like Winston—will have to carry a spare change of underwear. If you stay in school and do well, what do you have waiting for you after graduation? Why, a cubicle, of course, on the mauve walls of which you can hang the nonoffensive art item of your choice. And the longer you stay in school, the more likely it is that you will be sat on by Iggy or be humiliated by Xerxes. So, get out of school as quickly as you can. The longer you stay in, the more you will want to accomplish, and the worse off the rest of us will be.

"But, wait," you say. "I want to help my fellow humans. And I need to educate myself in order to do so." Let's say that you desire to develop a cure for cancer, that most evil of diseases. You do the following: go to school, study biology, get into a good college, study premed or biology there, get into a good medical school, gain acceptance to a really good postdoctoral program in oncology, and then work for a large drug company. Well, you do stand a good chance of actually helping to eliminate cancer.

But, consider...while you're busy doing all of that, the kid down the street, you know the one, with really short bangs who builds castles with his Legos, will decide that he wants to make his living by constructing buildings that have bad ventilation systems and lots of asbestos. While you're slaving away in med school over Petrie dishes and dreaming of a cancer-free world, your childhood friend will be sketching out blueprints for towers with asbestos-lined fire walls that would make I.M. Pei have a wet dream. Thus, all of your efforts will be for naught.

You and your elementary-school classmate will cancel out each other's efforts. But, if there were no school, then not only would there be no cancer-research industry, neither would there be cancer-producing industry. Remember, cancer, *the* disease of the twentieth century, is the result of uncontrolled growth and activity. When you have cancer, certain cells replicate endlessly until they eat the rest of your body. Just imagine each cell having a little to-do list on which there are thirty thousand entries. Each entry contains only one word: divide. If there were no school, there would be no cure for cancer, but then again we might not need one, because there would be very little heavy industry, which produces cancer in the first place. School, like smoking, is hazardous to your health. As is the case with smoking, it's best to quit before you become hooked.

§

Chapter 3:

The Myth of Work

Work sets us free, proclaims a sign at the front gate of a certain European ruin. We Americans work harder and longer than we ever have. But even when the economy booms, our salaries go into the crapper. Of course, we don't work just to pile up the filthy lucre. The sweat of our brows provides us not only with cash but also with our very identities. We work to earn self-respect, to establish our place in the community, to spiritually repay those who have given to us. As many multimillionaires gleefully exclaim, it's not about the money. We work to utilize our unique talents and to achieve self-actualization. (For a full listing of the benefits of work, see *Table Three*.)

Table Three: Selected Benefits of Work (Promised vs. Actual)

Promised Benefit	**Actual Benefit**
Challenging assignments	Bates-stamping
Interesting colleagues	People as pissed off as you are
Exciting opportunities for advancement	More Bates-stamping
Helpful and concerned mentors	Boss whose hero is Attila the Hun
Stimulating after-hours interaction with colleagues	Even more Bates-stamping

Please! Of course it's about the money. We work because we don't have the guts to go into something better and we work so hard because there are people with a vested interest in keeping us down, poor, and dumb. Work does not use our talents; it lays waste to our souls. Our employers tell us that we are all one big happy family in the workplace. Unfortunately, our work families are usually a cross between the Addamses and the Corleones. Entering the world of work at the age of twenty-two or twenty-three, young and idealistic, we leave it at sixty-five or seventy, used up like a snot-filled handkerchief. And that's what happens in the best of situations. Many of us, though, face other dilemmas.

For example, perhaps you have a younger boss, Alan, one of those Ivy-covered MBAs from Lower Merion, Pennsylvania. His favorite pastimes are biking, chanting, and driving up stock prices. While you enjoy playing a slow round of golf, he likes to bicycle up Mount Washington before breakfast. The handwriting is on the wall from the minute that your new—and so, so arrogant—supervisor arrives on the scene. Wearing a goatee and dressed in jeans, he informs you that the old ways don't cut the mustard anymore. Then he eyes your assistant, Eve, saying how wonderful she seems. Of course, you know that Eve is truly a goober. You've kept her on payroll only because you've felt sorry for her. After all, she has a mentally-retarded son who will be entering law-school soon.

One day Alan calls you into his office and says, "Wilbur, you're looking tired." You say that you're feeling better than you have in years. Alan says he's noticed that you're starting to slow down. "Of course," he says, "it's not any reflection on you personally. You're just not the worker you used to be."

"The hell I'm not," you reply, trying to sound confident, even though you're quaking inside. "I can do three times the work of someone half my age."

"It's no use," Alan says. "It's time for you to go. But don't worry, we're going to offer you a generous package."

You've seen these buy-outs before. "Yeah," you retort, "generous if my kids drop out of college and my wife and I stop eating."

With a charm cultivated by autumns spent at the *Wharton*

School of Business and summers in the Berkshires, Alan says, "Come on, Wilbur. You've played a good game. But now it's time to throw in the towel." He then offers you his hand, which you refuse. Twenty minutes later, you're being escorted out of the building by Security. The next week you hear from an old friend that Eve was given your job at about forty percent of your salary. You try to find other work, but you're too old to be useful. So, you spend the rest of your days dedicating yourself to the intricacies of philately.

This is one way in which you can leave the world of work. But there is another exit strategy as well. You attend your company's annual sales meeting, which is held in the employee cafeteria. Things are going better for the company than they ever have. Expenses are down, sales are up, and the net margin streaks into the stratosphere. You think to yourself that you're headed someplace. Well, you're at least partly right.

By way of celebrating the company's good fortune, Chad Gornick, the chief executive officer, duly decides that next year will be even better than this one. Gornick, though, doesn't think that operating revenues can be increased drastically. After all, the sales force has already exceeded goal by four-hundred percent. Many of the reps will use a large part of their bonus for convalescent leave and therapy expenses. So, if the company's net is really going to expand by the hoped-for ten percent, the growth must be gained from reduced expenses, not from increased revenue.

A task force commissioned by the CEO to study the conundrum has presented its findings. The company can't do much more than it already has in terms of reducing most of its expenses. It leases the cheapest property available in Venango County, Pennsylvania. The Judge Jack Lovell memorial warehouse makes the Triangle Waistcoat Company look like the Taj Majal. Moreover, the company currently crafts its product from the shoddiest materials that Chinese slave labor can provide. No, the panel concludes, there isn't much to be done on the general expense-reduction front. Composed of six senior managers and John Jenkins from the mail room, the committee decides that the requisite ten percent must be mined from salaries. But whose paychecks should be cut?

Debating at length, the committee looks at the various places from which fat can be trimmed. Several locations present themselves. First, there is senior management. The members of the committee consider this option—which is proposed by John from the mail room—for a full six seconds. They then discount it completely and vote to fire John on the spot for even thinking about such a ludicrous idea. The managers decide that they are, of course, much too valuable to the company to have their salaries trimmed. Their strategic marketing plans and the wonderful skits that they produce at the company's national sales meeting are far too important. No, they decide, you can't trim fat through decapitation. Besides, most of the senior managers own time shares in the Bahamas, and they can't possibly afford pay cuts this year. As for actually reducing their own number, well, that would be a ghastly thing to do, just ghastly. "We're all friends here," John Nesbitt says to his comrades. "Friends don't downsize friends." Nods and grunts of assent go around the oak conference-room table.

The task force then perfunctorily considers downsizing the sales department or perhaps reducing by a smidgen the rather generous incentive program enjoyed by the reps. But the committee is composed of former sales people. To tamper with the reps' compensation would be anathema. It would be like throwing away one's favorite prostitute. "Besides," argues the Director of Inside Sales, "if we cut the money that we give to the reps, what would their incentive be to do a good job? People need to have stars upon thars." On healthy bonus plans themselves, the people sitting around the table are in complete agreement. And so the compensation package offered to the reps will emerge unscathed from the ritual and financial bloodletting about to occur.

The final groups to be considered are production and development, the people who actually make the goods sold at outrageously expensive prices. Surely, they will be the last to put their necks on the block. Right? Wrong, about as wrong as it can get. As Chad Gornick says, "Grunt work and ideas are a dime a dozen. It doesn't matter how good the product is if we can't sell it. In fact, a good marketing campaign can sell anything."

It's therefore decided that half of the production department will be laid off and replaced by volunteers from a halfway house for people with profound metal disabilities. "It's not much of a stretch," John Nesbitt proclaims. "Most of the production department is profoundly fucked-up." The committee compliments itself on a job well done and adjourns to a French restaurant to enjoy a richly deserved fete, on the company expense account, of course. "Ah, thank heaven for the joys of a T&E voucher," says Nancy Jones, Vice President for New Ventures. She lights her cigarette with a crisp new one-hundred dollar bill.

As a result of the task force's work, the CEO announces that deep, deep cuts—strategic amputations, Gornick calls them—must be undertaken in order to save the company from financial atrophy. To emphasize the medical nature of the incisions, Gornick wears a surgical mask and rubber gloves as he reads the names of employees about to undergo a corporate biopsy.

You're a little stunned when you hear your name called out. As you stagger back to your cubicle to empty out your desk, you think about that new widget you designed last year. It made the company wads of money. You're sure of it. There must be a mistake somewhere. In desperation, you get on the computer and send a quick e-mail to the CEO, asking for clarification. In thirty seconds, a reply pops onto the screen. The subject of the electronic memo reads: "You have one hour to leave the company's premises." So, it's really no mistake. You're history. As you walk to the elevator, you see someone with profound Down's Syndrome being led into your cubicle. You've been downsized, baby.

Although many of us will be unceremoniously dumped when we have outlived our usefulness, many others will spend years working for somebody else before we're thrown out on our heads.

Let's take a look at a typical day in the life of a fast-track corporate worker. Lisa Jones is a marketing coordinator at Ishmael's Caffeine Machine, a young but very aggressive firm that competes against Starbucks. Ishmael's is headquartered on the twelfth to fifteenth floors of 501 Juniper St. in Boston. The company's motto is, "We fuel the corporate juggernaut. What about you?" Let's join Lisa as her day begins. When she climbs out of bed, she accidentally knees her sleeping boyfriend in the balls. "Too bad, kiddo," Lisa mumbles to the now-moaning Kurt. "I'm on my way to the top; you better get out of the road."

As she sleepily makes her way to the shower, she stops in the kitchen and flips on the switch of the coffee maker, the filter basket of which brims with *Tasmanian Devil*, a new coffee in the Warner Brothers line that she has helped to develop. She then goes to the bathroom and stands under the boiling water. After her shower, she dries herself off with one of the two three-hundred-dollar blue towels that she's bought from Macy's. She then returns to the bedroom, where Kurt has begun to snooze soundly again under the eight-hundred-dollar comforter from Nieman Marcus. Lisa is very proud of this item; it's one in a special series that Nieman had imported from Afghanistan before September Eleven: *Taliban Tidbits*. The comforter's certificate of authenticity specifies that it was made by a female Afghan doctor who was forced into embroidery work after the revolution. At least six cents of the purchase price went to a fund helping Afghan women to buy more-translucent veils.

On the wall opposite the armoire and the mirror in front of which she dresses is a giant framed poster that enjoins its reader to question authority. Lisa is very fond of the poster, which she bought from Bloomingdale's, for six-hundred dollars. The poster's message sums up her personality quite nicely: very cutting edge, very urban hip, very inquisitive. This she knows for the *Myers Briggs Type Inventory* that she took at Banana Republic told her so.

Lisa is very petite. She has achieved her physique through chain smoking, power walking, and drinking eight to ten double lattes a day. She's creative, too, very open to new ideas. And she's so thankful that her job at Ishmael's gives her the opportunity to question authority and to challenge mores. As she dresses in the new nine-hundred-dollar *Miss Che* miniskirt that she bought yesterday from Saks, she wonders why she always seems to get behind in her rent. That raise that she just received really doesn't stretch as far as she thought it would. Although Lisa makes a great deal of money now, over ninety thousand dollars a year, she doesn't see very much of it.

Lisa finishes putting on her *Anarchist's Pancake* makeup, and she walks out to the kitchen, where her coffee awaits. She pours some of the muddy mixture into the Ishmael's mug that she appropriated from work. Lisa loves the word "appropriate." It's just "so, so, appropriate," she told Kurt one morning. She adds about half a cup of milk to the coffee. Then she puts in three spoonfuls of sugar. And, just for good measure, she adds a shot of Glen Fiddich.

She sits down and takes a drink of the coffee; then she reaches into her purse and fishes out a pack of Virginia Slims. "Find your Voice," proclaims the logo on the back of the pack. This urging, which improved sales by thirty percent, was written by a chain-smoking copywriter who died three months ago from throat cancer.

Lisa usually gets started in the morning with two or three cups of coffee and five or six cigarettes. This mixture of caffeine and nicotine helps her to establish a baseline of stimulation that will propel her through her day like the corporate steamroller she is becoming.

Lisa's mind is already at work. Today she has to get the kinks out of a new product line that she's been developing. Ishmael's serves a very special market niche. About ninety-eight percent of the customers are college educated. And fully fifty percent have either graduate or professional degrees. As Madge Johnson, the national marketing manager and Lisa's immediate supervisor, says, "Our customers are smart, smart, smart. They're fast, fast, fast. They work, work, work." Madge prides herself on the fact that she drinks eleven-and-a-half cups of Ishmael's coffee a day. Madge has a blood pressure of 160/300. And her heart is ready to leap out of her rib cage. She smokes three packs of cigarettes a day, is on her fourth husband, and prides herself on being a liberated woman. Lisa hopes one day to become as successful as Madge.

And at the tender age of twenty-nine, Lisa is on her way. She's already careening down the fast track toward success and a double aneurysm. Every product line that Lisa has designed has been wildly successful. The only spot of tarnish on an otherwise impeccable record stems from the time she uttered a malapropism—"coffee line"—in the presence of Ishmael's CEO, Martha Little Sympathy, a former pot-head from Seattle.

Martha's surname used to be Goldblatt, but upon discovering that she was one-thirty-second Iroquois on her mother's side, she adopted a Native American moniker. Although Martha had been hesitant about the change at first, a close friend in PR assured Martha that Indian was definitely in. "Honey, any product even remotely connected to the Native American tradition is a surefire winner," said the friend, who had herself coined the brand name *Noble-Savage Breeder Reactors*.

When Lisa had said, "coffee line," Martha gently corrected her: "Product line, baby, product line. We want to be able to transfer our branding to any commodity that can give us the highest gross margin. Today it's coffee. But, who knows, tomorrow it could be electric chairs. Whatever gives us the highest income contribution is what we flog." So, suitably chastened, Lisa now religiously refers to all of Ishmael's brews as products. And despite her early linguistic mistake, Lisa's career moves quickly ahead.

When Lisa finally reaches Ishmael's this bright October morning, she prepares for her meeting with Martha Little Sympathy. Lisa has been Martha's protégé ever since she—Lisa—created the new "Warner Brothers Cartoon Nostalgia Line." Besides the *Tasmanian Devil AAA*, Lisa also developed *Daffy Duck Decaf* and *Bugs' Dark Roast.* Best of all, and what gave Lisa her promotion, was the phenomenal licensing agreement that she worked out with Warner Brothers. There were the normal cross-market promotions, of course: one could inexpensively purchase a Daffy Duck doll with a pound of Decaf or get a free doll after the purchase of seven large Decafs from retail stores within a three-week period. There was another aspect to the deal as well. A Warner Brothers artist added retroactive product placements to the old cartoons. When the anvil is about to dent the head of the Coyote, Wiley holds up a sign saying, "In the name of humanity, buy *Road Runner Robust.*" Martha Little Sympathy was ecstatic about the product placement. Until Lisa's idea, nobody had been able to penetrate the under-five coffee market. The "Coffee-Drinkers of Tomorrow," Martha had called them. The new Warner Brothers product line and subsequent advertising campaign were complete successes. Ishmael's profits rose by three-hundred percent in nine weeks. Starbucks was beginning to get nervous. Martha Little Sympathy celebrated the caffeinated triumph by building sweat lodges on each floor of Ishmael's. Today, during a strategic planning session to be held in the lodge outside Martha's office, Lisa is going to tell her boss about her newest idea.

"Martha," she asks her chief, whose pores are beginning to open, "when you think Starbucks, what image comes to mind?" Madge chants for a moment, invokes the East Wind, and says, "That hunky young guy, who was the friend of

Captain Apollo on *Battlestar Galactica*." Lisa has never seen the show in question, but she did get an "A" in her "Introduction to American Literature" class at Penn, which was taught by Professor Ryan, an aging professor and World War II veteran famous for being rescued from a small town French town, St. Raoul.

Lisa shakes her head slowly. Taking a long drag on the peace pipe that she keeps in the lodge, Madge smiles and says, "Okay, baby, I'll bite. What do you see?"

"*Moby Dick*."

"You mean the book about the whale? God, I slept through that thing. I remember that my English class was right before Marketing, where that cutey, David Smith, sat. Why do you think of *Moby Dick*?"

"Well, Starbuck was the first mate on the *Pequod*, Captain Ahab's ship. I always sort of thought that you named this company after Ishmael, the protagonist of the novel."

"Honey," Martha says, "this company is named after Ishmael Goldblatt, my third husband. I hated that fucker's guts."

"Why did you name the company after him if you hate him so much?"

"Out of spite. When you get to be my age, you'll learn that spite is as good a motive as any. The alimony money my lawyer got out of Ishmael provided the start-up cash for this company. I wanted the old shit to know that I was getting rich—with his money and his name. Success is the best revenge. That's the story behind Ishmael's. So, come on, sweetheart, tell your chief what your idea is."

"Martha, I know that our demographic niche is people in the top income brackets. And that kind of money generally means lots of expensive Ivy-League educations. Everybody who has been to college has read—" Lisa pauses for a second, nods deferentially to her chief, and continues, "at least slept through *Moby Dick*. So we have a line of coffee products..."

Martha smiles at Lisa's use of the word "product."

"Our customers will think that we're acknowledging their education and their savvy if we have a product line that uses names from the novel. In reality, we'll be manipulating them and aligning a work of art with corporate dreck, but hey, look how well *The Simpsons* did by making a few references to *The Seventh Seal.* Remember when Bart played a game of Twister with Death? I did my research. Their ratings went through the roof."

Lisa pauses for a second and takes a toke from the peace pipe that Martha passes to her. Lisa's head begins to spin after the first inhalation. "Hey, what's in this thing, Martha?"

"Hash from Morocco. Tomorrow, we're going to try peyote. My shaman says that hallucinogens help to open the mind for vision quest." Martha shivers for a second and calls to Sven, her Norwegian masseur. On orders from his boss, Sven wears only the face paint of an Iroquois warrior, moccasins, and a smile. "Sven, honey, pour some more water on the rocks. It's getting kind of cold in here. Besides, I think that we're really close to giving birth to a new product line. More steam, more steam, we need to open up Lisa's money center. Go on, baby. Tell Mama your idea."

Lisa's head really begins to swim now from the combined effects of the hash and the steam. She closes her eyes and sees Patrick Stewart standing at the helm of the Pequod during a storm. The ship dives into the water and then rides the crest of the wave, and then dives again into the next trough. In Ahab's left hand is the ship's wheel. In his right is a steaming cup of coffee. Ahab wears on his peg leg a wrap-around rotating sign with a blinking neon light. It says, "*Tashtego Tanzanian*, good enough to sail around Perdition's horn for, but you don't have to. Available exclusively from Ishmael's Caffeine Machine." The *Pequod* emerges from a trough, and Lisa sees that the wave is composed not of water, but of twenty dollar bills. She looks directly at Ahab, and she sees that the face is not Patrick Stewart's nor even Gregory Peck's, but her own. Lisa knows that she has had a vision. She will ride the caffeinated wave of money to the ends of the marketing world.

From far away, Lisa hears a gentle voice saying, "Honey, are you still there? Sven, she's kind of stoned. Why don't you give her a rub down?"

Lisa opens her eyes and sees the really cute Sven walking over to her and gently pushing her over on her stomach. As he starts pounding on her back, she says, "Martha, I've had my first real marketing vision. I can see it now: *Tashtego Tanzanian, The Harpooner's Hazelnut, Ishmael's Irish Cream*. We'll make millions."

"Ah," says Martha. "I knew that building a sweat lodge was a great idea. Baby, after your coup with the Warner Brothers line, I trust you. Maybe I can get the WB to write some product placements into *Moby Dick* for us." Lisa says that this retro placement would be a great idea. The tension in her shoulders melts away as Sven continues to work on her. Thus is born the *Moby Dick* product line.

After leaving the sweat lodge and coming down from her hash buzz, Lisa heads to a focus-group meeting that the New Ventures Department is running. Lisa loves these groups because they give her an opportunity to find out what's happening in the marketplace. It was in just such a group that she learned that coffee drinkers are quite likely to identify with Warner Brothers cartoon characters. On the other hand, people who drink soda and juice are, on the whole, much more likely to watch Disney cartoons.

Lisa walks up the stairs to the fourteenth floor and goes into the glass booth next to the room in which the focus group is being held. The booth has a window onto the focus-group room, and the subjects can be seen through a two-way mirror and heard through hidden microphones. When Lisa enters the booth, she finds Melissa Franklin monitoring Ferdinand Bandera, the third member of the focus-group task force. Ferdinand is taking the seven people in the group through what Ishmael's calls the tolerance questions.

It's through asking these questions that the company

accumulates the data that will enable it to both cut costs and raise prices. Sitting at the head of the table and holding a cup of coffee in his left hand, Ferdinand asks, "Okay, folks, how much is too much? How expensive would a cup of coffee have to be before you wouldn't buy it?" Ferdinand then takes the group through a range of prices. Six of the seven members beg off at around $3.50. Ferdinand is pleased, though, to find that one member—obviously a true coffee addict—would actually pay as much as $37.50 for a cup of java. And, the focus-group member adds, if the retail establishment in question takes American Express, he just might pay more.

Lisa leaves the booth and comes into the room to introduce herself. She then says, "Ferd, let me butt in for a minute." Lisa asks how much coffee people can drink before they start getting too dizzy to concentrate, before their heads start doing Linda Blair imitations. Most of the people in the room say that their tolerance is around eight cups a day. And Lisa is amazed by the answer of one of the people—Elizabeth Jenkins, an obstetrician on the night shift at the Bill Kroc Memorial Hospital of Medford Lakes, New Jersey. Elizabeth says that she can't do a C-section unless she has had at least four double lattes. She generally performs six premature deliveries a night, and if she doesn't tank up on coffee, her hands start to shake from caffeine withdrawal. Unfortunately, Elizabeth seems to be the exception rather than the rule. While the high-end group to which Elizabeth belongs will budget perhaps twenty dollars a day, most people, Lisa thinks, can afford around five bucks. And Lisa definitely wants Ishmael's *Tashtego Tanzanian* to dominate this mainstream market segment.

Lisa hopes that this focus group will give her information as helpful as that provided by the members of another group that she conducted last year for people on the low end of the market, the unemployed and those in dead-end jobs. When Lisa had first come up with the idea of a low-end coffee, *Prole-Slop*, Madge had said, "Lisa, it's not our demographic niche."

But Lisa had fought for the new product. A former link in the *Hands Across America* chain formed in 1986, Lisa is not merely a great marketer and product developer; she is also a social activist. "Look, Martha, poor people—as dirty and smelly as they are—have just as much of a right to a coffee buzz as we, the corporate movers and shakers, do. I'm serious about this, Martha," she had said, when she and Madge had met with Little Sympathy. "I want Ishmael's to be a coffee with a conscience."

"Sure, Honey, but just don't tell that to the pickers in Mexico that we pay two dollars a week to," Martha had said.

"Well, duh!" Lisa had replied. "I know that we really have to underpay the pickers, but we do give them six free cups of Ishmael's a day. Business is business. And I think that we can make a seventy-nine percent net profit on *Prole-Slop*." Martha had said that as long as the company raked in the cash, she didn't see a problem with caffeinating the great unwashed, provided that they stood downwind. And so *Prole-Slop* was launched. Sold in little white recyclable cups with black fists on them, it turned out to be very popular with students at Yale and Vassar. In fact, it became downright hip to be seen with a cup of *Prole-Slop* in one's hand. And in order to tap into the African-American market, Lisa launched an advertising campaign showing Malcolm X drinking a cup of *Prole-Slop* that had been air-brushed into his fist.

Now, though, Lisa is very interested in the responses of the focus group to the next question put to them by Ferdinand: "What products do you most associate with coffee?" The majority of the people reply, "Cigarettes." Lisa already knows about the strong correlation between the two products.

The next commodity cited is "books." "Aha," thinks Lisa, "I'm on to something here." She says, "What I would like you to tell me is how you feel when you drink coffee. What word most describes qualities you associate with coffee drinkers?"

Some say, "Smart." Others say, "Productive." And still others say, "Studious and alert." Lisa smiles at the responses;

they're exactly what she wants to hear. She asks one final question. "When I say classic literature, what first comes to mind?" One respondent, Brian, an aging stock broker, mentions *Playboy*. Seeing the looks of disapproval on the faces of his fellow focus-group members, he blushes and changes his answer to *The Wall Street Journal*. Another respondent, a caffeinated Unitarian minister, names *Self-Reliance*. The rest reply as Lisa knew they would: *Moby Dick*. That clinches it for the establishment of the new product line.

Lisa lets Ferdinand finish putting the group through its paces. And then she goes down to spend the rest of the afternoon as a management representative to the Worker Empowerment Training session. Mandatory, these sessions are designed, as their name suggests, to empower workers. She arrives at the session, which is held in the McChristian Conference Lounge, a windowless room containing an oblong table with twelve chairs on each side.

The empowerment sessions have not been going particularly well lately, since one person in the advertising copy department has been rather snotty. Todd, a young writer, had said that the sessions merely empower him to work longer hours for the same crappy pay. According to Todd, who spends his evenings reading the works of *The Frankfurt School*, empowerment has a great deal to do with a livable wage and good working conditions, maybe even stock options. "I'm alienated from the fruits of my labor," the angry Todd told William Steptoe, his direct supervisor.

William later communicated to Martha Little Sympathy that Todd had even intimated that he might try to unionize the department. "I'd fire him on the spot," William said. "But he's a really good writer. And he works his butt off."

Martha Little Sympathy consulted about the problem with her medicine man, Jonathan Running Scared. After three days spent ruminating, fasting, and chanting on a mountain in Washington, the Indian wise man delivered his pronouncement to Martha via cell phone: "The way that can be collectively bargained is not the true way. Try the Pinkertons."

Martha knew that Ishmael's needed Todd, but certainly not at the cost of a raise or unionization. If she gave in to Todd's demands, she might have to pay other workers more money just for their efforts. No, this simply would not do. There was something un-American about the idea. The key, Martha felt, was to make the workers grateful for being treated abhorrently, to make them feel damn glad that they even had jobs. After all, writers, even the best ones, are a dime a dozen.

In accordance with Martha's instructions, each member of the copy-writing staff has received a special day-long empowerment/reeducation session. And Todd's session is today. For thirteen hours, he has been allowed to drink only Earl Grey tea. He sits by himself on one side of the table, and on the other side sit twelve glaring managers, who are rotated every two hours so that a fresh contingent is always available. For the session's first eight hours, the management teams poke holes in Todd's work. This is actually very hard to do since his writing for Ishmael's is practically flawless.

Finding nothing wrong with his current work, the committee makes use of intelligence gathered by its Sociological Department. Special agents went to Todd's ninth-grade English teacher, Mrs. Flatley. Under the influence of three-hundred dollars in cash, Mrs. Flatley recalls that Todd had a great deal of trouble with homonyms. Often he would confuse T-H-E-I-R with T-H-E-R-E.

"Ah-ha," says Melanie Bunch, a Vice President in Corporate, "I just knew that you were a fuck-up, you little weasel." The committee has brought Todd to the point at which he is ready to admit that he may occasionally use "importantly" incorrectly. The committee believes that Todd will crack soon. And it prepares to hit him with a coup-de gras.

Using information that it has obtained from his parents, the committee spends two hours asking Todd why it should continue to employ someone who is obviously such an awful son. Todd's mother told Mumford Lewis from the Sociological Department about the time that Todd accidentally poisoned the family dog when he was a child.

"Well," says one of the committee members, "even when you were a kid, you were demonstrating pathological tendencies. Are you going to try to poison your supervisors?"

"It was an accident," Todd says. "I didn't know that Drano was poisonous. I just thought that the pretty blue crystals would add some color to Fido's food. I didn't know that the stuff would hurt the dog. I loved my dog. How did you find out about this?"

"We're your employers, Todd. We know everything about you. We just want you to be honest with yourself and to admit how bad of a person you can be."

Todd's mind is reeling, and his eyes are smarting because he's been made to stare into a Kleig light all day. Bill Fokker, the human resources manager, sees Todd beginning to cry and makes his move: "We know that you dislike your parents and that this antipathy has been sublimated into rebellion against the company. We are, after all, the ultimate in locos parentis. Give into Ishmael's, Todd, and you'll be happy again. You don't want to do any of that nasty collective bargaining. We know that you don't. It doesn't make you feel very good. You know that you'd rather work for the good of the company, and we'll give you the tools that you need to succeed. So, follow our lead, and you'll be incredibly happy. Just work hard, and never, ever, question your betters."

During the short break before the final session, Bill tells Lisa, who will direct Todd's interrogation, about the progress that they have made so far. "Lisa," he says to his comrade in coercion, "we've done all the negative work we can. We've undermined his authority to judge his own work. We've made him think of his own political rebellion as a manifestation of a father-child power struggle. We've made him think that he's really immature for daring to assert himself against our authority. We've also shown him that the only way forward—

from a psychological perspective—is for him to redouble his efforts in service to the company and to accept a slight pay cut as punishment for his resistance. This is the only way that he can make amends for the trouble that he's caused us. Now, Lisa, what you need to do is to plant in his mind the seed of a new project, something that he can give his entire life and all his energy to."

Lisa is thinking of the *Moby Dick* product line. While she's great at brainstorming broad brush-stroke ideas, she's never been very good at actually developing detailed proposals. So, when it's her turn to sit at the table, she chooses a seat directly across from Todd. Lisa looks into Todd's bloodshot, vacant eyes and says, "Todd, I have a solution to your problem. You can feel good about yourself only if you spend the next year working unsparingly on the advertising campaign for *Moby Dick* Coffee. You want to feel good about yourself, don't you? You want to feel as if you have a sense of purpose, don't you?"

"Yes, ma'am," he answers in a voice that sounds as if the speaker is on Quaaludes. Actually, the committee has been spiking the Earl Grey tea.

Lisa tells Todd about the project. And then, following Bill's suggestions, she says, "Doesn't it sound like fun to work on this campaign?"

"Yes, ma'am, it does," Todd says. And a little light returns to his eyes.

"Well, you little shit. We're not going to let you work on it unless you beg us. If you don't work on this project, you're never going to be happy, and you've been so rebellious that we don't think you deserve to be allowed to work on it."

Todd has broken down completely by this point and is ready to be empowered in whatever manner the committee deems appropriate. He begs Lisa to be allowed to write copy for the *Moby Dick* line. Lisa teases him, thinking that this empowerment training is almost as much fun as sex. In fact, she thinks that she'll try to use some of the techniques she has learned here on Kurt.

Finally, at the end of the session, Lisa allows Todd to participate in the project. He falls down on his knees and thanks her for the privilege of being able to continue to work at Ishmael's on a reduced salary. The other managers congratulate Lisa on a job well done. It's the end of the day, and Lisa rushes out to her health club.

Thus is the story of Ishmael's. The *Moby Dick* product line is a smash hit. Ishmael's Caffeine Machine increases its market share and drives Starbucks to the edge of bankruptcy. Lisa is promoted again. The nation's collective heart rate skyrockets. Todd receives another pay cut.

Does this scenario sound healthy to you? Of course it doesn't. Work is not really a good thing. It's a place in which you perform a whole lot of labor for not very much in return. And even if you do get a decent salary, the only way you can make real money is to make people buy things that they really don't need. Do good work, do it efficiently, and you'll probably be laid off. There ain't no guarantee of nothing no mo'. Baby, the social contract is definitely broken.

What Not To Do:

Even though most of us will have to work for pay at some point in our lives, there are some concrete steps that you can take to make circumstances at least a little better.

1. Don't work very hard.

Spend most of your time goofing off and sucking up to those in authority. Hey, just remember, it's not what you know, but who you know that's really important.

2. Live at home and sponge off your parents as long as you can.

What's the oldest you should be before you get your own place? Twenty? Thirty? Maybe fifty? Do your darnedest to stay at home as long as you possibly can. Is it really goofing off? Is it really sponging off your parents? Well, maybe it is, but if your parents are with it, they'll understand why you want to stay in your room all the time. Hey, they weren't able to avoid the world of work. But if you stay at home, maybe you can. That's what America's all about: each generation being a little better off than the one that came before.

3. Don't play it safe at work.

The really depressing fact is that most of us will spend a great deal of our lives working to make other people rich. A job is generally a life sentence. There is one way out, though, if you're brave enough to take it. Workplace injuries often bring with them monetary compensation. Self-inflicted injures may be just the ticket out of the world of labor you've been looking for. Sure, it might hurt when you stick your hand in the paper shredder. But what's a little pain for a few hours compared with the years of drudgery that you can avoid simply by flinging yourself down a flight of stairs.

As soldiers in World War I knew, there are only three ways to escape the front. One consists of waiting until the end of the war. Well, your need to work isn't likely to end anytime soon. The second way is through death. Consider retirement to be your death, the end of your working life. The third way is to receive the golden wound, one so severe that it makes the recipient unfit for duty. Head for that paper shredder, baby.

§

Chapter 4:
The Myth of Mythology

As Thomas Hobbes once said, life is nasty, brutish, and short. As soon as you're born, you begin competing for scarce commodities: your parents' affection, praise from others, and dates with the sexy. Upon graduation from college, you perform mind-numbing labor that makes others rich and you neurotic. You keep busy after work in those few spare hours at your disposal by getting married and raising a couple of kids. And then you ease out of employment and into the joys of Alzheimer's as an inmate of the Little Step-Sisters of Mercy Nursing Home.

Most people don't go postal, though. They find other ways to keep themselves functioning. Some take drugs. Others watch television. Still others have lots of kinky sex. While all of these coping strategies provide benefits, none of them is as effective as the development of a belief system. Faith in something helps you to think that the tasks you perform on a daily basis actually have a purpose. If you're being exploited at work, you can—instead of unionizing—say that God is testing you through the nastiness of your employer. If your house explodes because of a leaky gas pipe—the seal of which a worker forgot to tighten because he was thinking about how nice his new jeans look—you can say that a higher power wants you to live more simply. All events, say believers, happen for a reason.

Like underwear, beliefs come in all shapes and sizes. Some believe in hard work, most especially when others are performing it. Others, concerned citizens that they are, believe in political action, as long is it doesn't affect the Net Asset Value of their mutual funds. Still others believe in that old standby, love, especially when dirty pictures are involved. But there's one object of belief that causes the most damage: God. (For a list of nine names for God through the ages, see *Table*

Four.) People who believe in God are often able to overcome insurmountable obstacles and to accomplish impossible tasks. But there are reasons why obstacles are insurmountable. And many tasks should be impossible.

Table Four: Nine Names for God throughout the Ages

Name
Yahweh
Allah
Imhotep
Buddha
Shiva
Bill Gates
Jesus
George Burns
Elvis

Let's take a brief stroll through the end of eleventh century and examine the case of Brother Raoul, a monk whose faith in God made him attempt a seemingly impossible task and allowed him to cause quite a bit of damage in the process. It's a Thursday afternoon in the High Middle Ages. Raoul, an enterprising young man in the French town of Clermont, has just embarked on his new career of pickpocket. His prospects look very good since his most important professional rival, Martin, has just been hanged. To make matters even more auspicious, there's a religious convention in town; rumor has it that the Holy Father himself will be arriving in a few hours. Business always perks up when the Church pays a visit.

Raoul doesn't realize that the meeting about to occur is not just another occasion to work out the intricacies of infant damnation. No, the Pope is arriving on this day in 1095 not to talk about limbo, but to preach Crusade. It seems that the pesky Muslims near Jerusalem are slitting Christian throats again. Moreover, the knights of Christendom were tamed by the Truce of God twenty years before. But they're getting a little bored. In search of action, they have begun using peasants as targets during lance practice. Farm production has dropped by seventy-five percent, and the situation approaches a crisis.

The Pope has decided to solve both problems by proclaiming a Crusade to the Holy Land. All of the knights—and anybody else who wants to pick up a sword—will have their sins forgiven if they merely go to the Levant and skewer Persians instead of peasants. The Pope believes that he has all of his bases covered. He gets those thuggish nobles out of his own backyard for a while, and the peasants can resume the work of growing their food and paying their tithe. Ten percent of a dead peasant isn't worth very much. Finally, the Holy Father will get to show those damn sultans who the real boss is.

During the afternoon of the Pope's arrival, Raoul works diligently at his trade. He surreptitiously removes two gold coins from the robe of a monk. Raoul sees monks as part of the biggest fraud he's ever encountered. They forgive the townsfolk's sins at the charge of five gold pieces for a venal sin and ten for a mortal. Then they sleep with most of their confessees, both female and male. When Raoul sees a monk, he knows that he views a colleague.

After making the monk a few ounces lighter, Raoul steals a very nice dagger from the belt encircling the major girth of a minor noble. He's about to take a bag of gold from the clutches of a large-bosomed woman, but then he hears the blowing of a trumpet and sees the Papal procession move into the square. The throng parts to allow the Pope and his entourage to pass. Raoul's stunned by the magnificence surrounding the Pontiff, especially by the Pope's jewel-encrusted shepherd's crook—the crook by which the flock of Christ is led. "That stick would keep me in wine for at least ten years," the pickpocket thinks to himself.

Raoul quickly formulates a plan to steal the crook. He'll dress in the robe of one of the monks and walk up for a Papal blessing. Then, he'll grab the crook and run like hell before anyone in the Pope's party can catch him. He leaves the big-bosomed woman alone and goes in search of a robe. As he passes an alleyway, he sees a monk taking a piss and swaying from the effects of too much sacramental wine. Raoul quickly walks up to the friar, who is mumbling the "Our Father" to himself in bad Latin, and hits the priest over his cowled head. The priest exclaims, "Dear Lord" and passes out. Raoul quickly strips the rotund friar and dons the robe and cowl. Then he steps out from the alleyway and into the crowd.

As Raoul makes his way to the platform, the Pope is addressing the faithful: "My people, we have come to a point in our lives as Christians at which we must live up to our beliefs. For too long now, we Christians have made a habit of fighting one another and not respecting ourselves as children of God. The time has arrived when we—especially the soldiers among us—must fight the true enemy, the heathen Muslim who threatens our very way of existence, who threatens to steal from us even the Holy Land of our Christ."

The crowd roars at the mention of the Holy Land. About fifty feet away from the Pope, Raoul thinks: "This guy can really work a crowd. I'd give anything to be able to do what he does."

The Pope waits until the cheering and roaring die down before continuing: "My children, anyone who takes up the sword and fights for Christendom and against the Heathen will have his sins forgiven." There is a great deal of polite clapping. The Pope changes tactics: "Not only that, but he won't have to pay his tithe while he's on Crusade." The crowd becomes ecstatic. By this point, Raoul is very close to the Pope. While the crowd roars again, Raoul makes a dash for the crook and grabs it. The Pope snaps his fingers, and several guards close in around Raoul. The Pope suddenly says, "Silence, my children." A hush falls over the crowd. Raoul realizes that everyone is looking at him and that he's probably going to be swinging from the end of a rope by nightfall.

The Pope cries out: "Look, my children, one of you, one of your poor, humble priests of the Lord will be the one to take up the crook of God and lead you to Jerusalem. What is your name, my brother?"

The stunned pickpocket responds: "Brother Raoul, Holy Father."

The Pope again shouts: "Look, my children. Brother Raoul will be the one to preach the Crusade and lead you to the Holy Land."

The crowd begins to chant: "Ra-oul, Ra-oul, Ra-oul."

The Pope leans in close to Raoul and whispers: "Thought you were going to pull a fast one, didn't you? I sure fixed your wagon. Now, you're either going to lead the Crusade, or I'll let them tear you apart. It's your choice." Raoul has to think only for a moment.

Three months later, Raoul is leading a band of fifteen thousand quite filthy mercenaries through a desert in the Levant. He's found that being a Crusade leader isn't really bad work. There's plenty of wine, he gets to ride in a cart, and he has to preach only twice a week. In fact, he actually begins to believe that he is an emissary of God, that he will be able to do anything if only he has faith in Christ.

One day, the group of Crusaders finds itself short of food and wanting to test its strength. Raoul tells his flock that it should attack a walled city on the horizon.

"But they have massed archers," complains one of the Crusaders, Sir Victor the Reluctant. "And we won't have any shelter. They'll kill us all."

Raoul is a little buzzed from wine and ready to do some hard-core preaching. He stands up in the cart and shouts to his flock: "My children, do you think that soldiers of Christ such as ourselves should be stopped by a mere wall and mere arrows?"

The flock joyfully answers its pastor: "No, Brother Raoul."

The pickpocket again queries the troops: "Do you want to prove yourself worthy of being soldiers of Christ? Or do you want to cower in fear, as Sir Victor the Reluctant would have you do?"

"We want to prove ourselves, Brother Raoul. We love you."

A little overwhelmed by the cheers of the crowd, Raoul replies: "I love you, too. Onward! Let us take this town in the name of God."

The crowd roars again, and with Brother Raoul in the lead, charges off toward the castle in the distance.

Inside the stronghold, two Muslim soldiers see the crowd rushing toward them. One of them sighs, "Not more Crusaders, that's the third batch this month. Why do they have to shout so loudly? Christians always give me a headache." He sounds a trumpet, and volleys of arrows fly out from the castle. Within twenty minutes most of the Crusaders are dead. Raoul came to his senses at the last minute and hid himself under the body of Sir Victor.

Because of the machinations of one monastic poseur, thousands believed that they could accomplish the impossible. And they were wrong. (For a list of seemingly impossible tasks accomplished through adherence to a religious belief system, see *Table Five*.)

Table Five: Seven Seemingly Impossible Tasks Accomplished Through Adherence to Religious Beliefs

Belief System	Seemingly Impossible Task Accomplished
Shinto	Rape of Nanking
Roman Catholicism	Getting people to take guys in silly hats seriously for 2000 years
Judaism	Morally justifying Israeli brutalizing of Palestinians
Scientology	Revitalizing John Travolta's acting career
Protestantism	Convincing fifteen generations of Africans that slavery is will of God
Hare Krishna	Making people like soy milk
Christian Science	Popularizing belief that childhood ailments should be treated by speaking in tongues rather than administering antibiotics

What not to do.

Clearly, belief in God—or whatever you call the divine watchmaker—can be very harmful. There are, however, some steps that you can not take in order to ensure that you and your loved ones don't fall into the grip of the theologians.

1. Don't send your children to summer Bible camp.

Few religious zealots started their lives as true believers. Rather, they were socialized into their zealotry through attending a variety of religious events, such as summer Bible camp. You may think to yourself, "Well, it seems pretty harmless, singing a few verses of 'Kumbya' and drinking a little Kool-Aid. What's so bad about that?" Sure, these events may seem innocent enough, but they were exactly the program of the day at Jonestown in 1978. Just imagine the Reverend Jim Jones sitting around in the jungles of Guyana, strung out on painkillers, and wailing: "Drink the Kool-Aid, my children. The Lord is coming. Just drink the Kool-Aid." Nip this kind of tragedy in the bud by encouraging your children to play video games during their summer vacations. Sure, Nintendo doesn't allow for much socializing, but neither does it lead to death in the jungle.

2. Don't listen to sacred music.

Have you ever listened to Gregorian chants? If you have, you might have thought that the music seemed beautiful and other worldly. But what most people don't realize is that the chants are just part of a whole package. Along with the chants come wearing hair shirts, taking vows of poverty, and sleeping in an unheated dormitory room with twenty or thirty other guys who haven't gotten laid in twenty years. Sound good to you? Chant away, baby.

3. Don't take sacred books literally.

Picture this: a tome just brimming with sex, violence, and irrationality. What's the title? *A Hundred and Twenty Days of Sodom*? *Penthouse*? *Reader's Digest*? Actually, the book in question is the Old Testament. Before reading the Bible, ask yourself a question. What kind of world do you want? One in which people who happen to lust after those of their own gender are stoned to death in the public square? A world in which women with the potential to save lives as surgeons are relegated to saying the rosary while dressed as penguins? A world in which people find the faith to do well on the stock market and believe in lethal injection? If you read the Bible and believe in it literally, this world can be yours.

§

Chapter 5:
The Myth of Self-Actualization

Although it's understandably quite difficult to see this fact through the smoke drifting up from what used to be the World Trade Center, religion has taken a back seat to politics, economics, and self-actualization in the twenty-first century. As Friedreich Nietzsche proclaimed shortly before he went off his rocker in the last part of the nineteenth century, God is dead. Unfortunately, Osama Bin Laden wants the rest of to be as well.

Minding the store in God's place are economists, politicians, and the gurus of the self-help movement. We'll focus on the first two another time. For right now, the latter are quite enough. The zeal with which these gurus preach their message is every bit as intense as that exhibited by the Pope and Raoul. But the goal of the gurus' preaching is both similar to and different from that espoused by our two medieval Christians. Not only do the preachers want to fatten their own wallets, they also want their clients to find—not God—but "it." What is it? How does one discover it?

In order to answer these questions, let's move from Europe of the Middle Ages to America of the 1970s. Our visit to the polyester decade will enable us to see the way in which one person, William Ginley, finds "it" at a meeting of the group that our Lincoln dealer, Dave, visited in the introduction.

A very minor explosion in the postwar baby boom, Ginley dropped out of his mother's womb in 1947 and out of Cal State Bakersfield in 1967. From 1968 to 1975, the same period during which Mr. Xerxes was gleefully planting land mines on the Ho Chi Minh Trail, Ginley was in Philadelphia, engaged in that odd business of finding himself. For Ginley, finding himself consisted mainly of allowing his hair to resemble that worn by the Germanic Barbarians lamented of by Boethius in *Consolations of Philosophy*. Ginley also did much soul-searching in coffee houses frequented by long-legged, sharp-cheeked, and chain-smoking girls who loved long-haired guys. In addition to leaving no stone unturned in this search, Ginley also turned down no opportunity to get stoned. Years later, Ginley would tell his friends what a wonderful period of time it was, with so much political change in the air. Actually, for Ginley, the only odor wafting through his immediate neighborhood was the sweet smell of cannabis.

In June of 1978, Ginley realized that he had somehow turned twenty-eight and was still spending most of his time sleeping off being stoned at a West Philadelphia squat called the Puncture Palace. Ginley had just mentally unpacked after a quite-bizarre acid trip in which he had—in the body of a pterodactyl and the voice of J. R. Johnson—been the featured contestant on *The Gong Show*: "You can call me Ptero, you can call me Dactyl. Just don't call me Pterodactyl."

Ginley decided upon his return that he had to find a purpose in life. A few days after his horrifying trip, he was lounging on a hammock strung across the porch of the Puncture Palace. As he watched a garbage truck pass by, a really beautiful young woman, Heather, walked onto the porch. She lived next door to the Palace and worked as a production assistant for a small film company. Heather invited Ginley to attend an event downtown entitled "The Formula." When Ginley replied—only half-jokingly—that he might consider going if hospitality bowls would be provided, she said that he just didn't get it. But, she suggested, he might get it if he came with her. And, she said, getting it would change his life. After considering that his schedule was free until October of 1987, and simultaneously undressing her with his eyes, he thought that if he didn't get it, he might, at the very least, get laid, so, he agreed to attend The Formula.

The next day he accompanies Heather to a large hotel in Center City. All the participants of that day's session of The Formula—about three or four hundred of them—are milling around at the entrance to a conference room, which contains hundreds of straight-backed chairs arranged in ranks and files. Some of the people, most of whom are middle aged, and at least half of whom are women, wear little name tags that say "Coach." At the front of the windowless conference room is a raised platform on which stand a podium and a director's chair. Behind the platform is draped a huge banner, upon which is printed in black letters a message informing people that "***IT'S ALL WORTHLESS***." Another banner reads: "***The Formula is that THERE IS NO FORMULA***." Smaller signs placed at strategic locations around the room carry other cryptic messages, such as "***I CREATE IT ALL***" and "***BE IT***" and "***THROW IT AWAY***." Luckily for Ginley, there are no Dixie cups containing cyanide-laced Kool-Aid.

When Ginley and Heather walk into the room, Heather strides over to a large man in a white t-shirt and black pants who stands near a cash box. Heather says, "It's okay, he's with me. I just made quota this month." The man's biceps are the size of small watermelons. He nods. Heather turns to Ginley and says, "It's free the first time you come with a member of the group. But when you decide to come back, it costs you fifty dollars."

"That's a pretty high price," Ginley says.

"Not when you get it," retorts Heather, with a sleepy smile on her face. They walk over to a rectangular table, and Heather picks up a laminated white name card that's on a string and that has a caption that reads, "I'm a coach." Heather hangs the sign around her neck; then she selects a blank card, writes Ginley's name on it, and slips the noose over his head. Although Ginley really doesn't really like wearing name tags, he does really dig being touched by Heather, and he figures that he'll be able to score after he discovers what it is.

Just as Ginley and Heather finish labeling themselves, a man dressed in a black turtleneck shirt comes to the podium and says, "Remember, these sessions usually last eight hours. And we don't open the door until we're finished. So, if you need to get a quick snack or to use the facilities, you have to go now. Once we start, we won't stop until you get it." A small titter arises from people at the use of the last three words. The man continues: "Just remember that we don't allow food or drink during the session, so you have to eat outside. And hurry up. Zack'll be coming up on stage in exactly six minutes." Ginley and Heather repair to the snack table immediately outside the conference room. The table offers famished seekers yogurt and yak milk.

"Not much of a selection," Ginley complains.

"It's enough to fill you up," Heather says, and she adds, "Zack likes things that begin with 'Why'." Ginley is impressed by this quasi-mystical answer, which, as he later learns, was dreamt up by a marketing executive who vowed to commodify the known universe.

Ginley and Heather wolf down their food and return to their seats. When Ginley asks Heather why no one is allowed to leave the room during the session, Heather says that it's not possible to get it while being focused on things that aren't it. Ginley is feeling both slightly nauseated by the yak milk and mildly horny after having rubbed up against Heather. He's under the mistaken impression, shared by millions of his fellow humans, that tautology and non-sequitur, if said often enough, are really profundity. "What is it?" he asks.

Heather replies, "You'll only know when you get it." Ginley nods sagely, without having the slightest idea of what she's talking about.

Suddenly the doors shut with a bang. Two large men with suspicious bulges under their armpits slide in front of the exit. The lights blink out, and gasps go up from the crowd as the room is plunged into utter blackness. A spotlight focuses on a tall blond man dressed in a black t-shirt, wide red suspenders, and dark aviator sunglasses. He speaks into a microphone that he holds in his hand and that's hooked up to a reverberation system. "It's all worthless," he says. The last word bounces off the walls: "worthless, worthless, worthless." For two full seconds after the word finishes boinging around the room, the crowd sits in silence. Then, a very thin woman in her mid-thirties with long brown hair flowing straight down her back, shouts: "You're right. It's all worthless!" Another voice joins the first: "It's not worth a goddamn thing." A third voice chimes in, and a fourth, and then a cacophony of voices starts howling about the lack of value in anything. Some people stand bolt upright, inadvertently kicking over their chairs. Others simply throw themselves down on the carpeted floor and writhe. All the while Zack sits smiling silently on his director's chair.

Suddenly, Zack jumps to his feet, points at a person rolling around on the floor and shrieks: "You don't get it." Zack pulls off his sunglasses and casts his gaze around the room: "None of you gets it. I'm going to show you how to get it. But most of you will never get it. You might as well just throw it away and forget it."

At this last proclamation, a woman runs toward the stage, shouting, "I love you, Zack. Please help me to get it. I'll never get it without you." As she approaches the stage with the zeal of a fanatic, two beefy security guards grab her (one under each arm) and carry her away to the back of the conference room.

Then Zack, with his white teeth sparkling in the spotlight, speaks once again to the crowd: "Here's the secret: Let it go, throw it away. Then create it: be it." Nods, hallelujahs, and hosannas go around the room. "Coaches, pair up with the neophytes. Just do it. I'll return in two hours to see who's got it, who doesn't have it, and who's really going to get it." He then displays a smile that would be quite at home on the Cheshire Cat.

The spotlight winks out. For a second, the room descends once more into the abyss of darkness. Then the lights come back on. Ginley sits in his chair in a state of shock. Although he's beginning to suspect that Zack's full of it, he still has no concrete idea of what it might be. The man in a turtleneck returns to the stage. "You heard Zack: Coaches, partner up with the new folks. New guys, you're really in for it, so get ready to give it all up. If you coaches need any assistance, just raise your hand, and one of the staff members will be right over to help you with it."

Ginley notices that next to the podium now stands a phalanx of rather large and menacing men and women wearing close-cropped hair and black t-shirts. They resemble the aides of the Penguin on *Batman*, except that they don't have names such as "Biff," "Boff," or "Bingo" emblazoned across their chests in yellow letters. With bowels that desperately desire to move the yogurt, Ginley turns to Heather and says, "I need to take a dump."

Heather's face has gone blank. She reminds Ginley that there will be no bathroom breaks. Instead of worrying about relieving himself, he should shut up, stand up with his arms at his side, and turn toward her. A little shocked and regretting that he consumed the yak milk, Ginley does as he's told. Heather looks into his eyes, gives him a small and strange smile, and then shouts: "You're worthless!" Ginley's bloodshot eyes almost pop out of their cavernous sockets. Heather continues: "You're a pot-smoking hippy freak who does absolutely nothing. Why don't you just give it all up?"

From around the room similar shouts can be heard. And Ginley begins to wonder if an afternoon at The Formula is too high of a price to pay for a sexual encounter with Heather. For the next hour or so, Heather tells Ginley that he's completely worthless, that he doesn't get it, and that he needs to get his head out of his butt. Ginley just thinks, "This is a sick joke." He attempts to fend off Heather's verbal blows as best he can. Although Heather tells him to maintain eye contact with her, he sees two of the Penguin's female helpers carry away a woman with flailing arms. She has just said to her coach, "Stick it up your ass." The helpers disappear with the resistant participant into a small chamber off the side of the main room. After ten minutes or so, the woman, on wobbly knees and with helpers gently guiding her by the elbows, retakes the floor.

He hears the woman say to her coach, "You're right, I just didn't get it. But I'll try to get it now." Ginley doesn't want to find out what's in the side room. He figures that he'll simply say whatever Heather wants him to. Then he'll go home and smoke some pot.

Ginley tries to maintain the small sense of self that he has left. But after an hour of being told that he doesn't get it, he starts to waver. He thinks that maybe Heather's right, that he just doesn't get it, that he'll never get it, that Yak milk isn't so bad.

Then the seminal moment arrives. Heather asks him what he wants to be. Although Ginley's tempted to say, "Napping," he realizes that such a response would evoke another blood-curdling shout. Instead, he casts around in his cobwebbed mind for a suitable answer. Two weeks before he came to The Formula, one of his squat mates ran a clandestine line from the power pole across the street and delivered the joys of unpaid-for electricity to the squat. Another housemate had found in the basement an old TV set. He dragged it up into the living room, and placed it under the most sacred spot in the house—the wall that displayed a Jim Morrison poster.

That night Ginley and his squat mates had been smoking some very impressive hash, eating popcorn, and watching the grand old television. They had viewed an episode of *Star Trek* in which Jim, Spock, and Bones had to soothe a pregnant and animated pile of concrete: "Pain, eternity, it ends," mimicked the household electrician. And another housemate said, "Jim, I'm not a brick layer, I'm just an old-fashioned country doctor." Ginley had always liked Bones. He seemed so together, and the Intergalactic attending always wore a natty smock. Whenever Jim and Spock were down on the planet getting eaten by nasty man-size lizards, Bones was back up in Sick-Bay, safe and sound. More important, Dr. McCoy was always helping people, whereas Jim and Spock and Scotty were always blowing them up.

"A doctor," Ginley says with a slight smile on his face,

hoping to avoid additional nastiness on the part of Heather.

"A doctor?" Heather asks. "They help people. What do you know about helping anybody except yourself?"

Ginley had read *Arrowsmith* during his first and only semester at Cal State Bakersfield and remembered Marty's attempt to find a cure for the plague. "Maybe I can help to relieve people's suffering."

Heather slaps Ginley on the cheek and admonishes him: "Throw it away, and just be it."

Realizing that his life up to this point, while fairly pleasurable, has not been productive, Ginley vows that he will become a doctor. A Zen-like awakening, unheard of even on the pages of D.T. Suzuki, spreads over him: "I've got it," he says, with a zeal similar to that once found at Masada just before the Romans broke down the doors and found the fortification's inhabitants rather permanently indisposed. "I can let it all go now, I can embrace it, and I can really be it."

He begins to cry and to believe that, despite fainting at the sight of blood, he would be a great doctor. After all, he could get his nurse to deal with the messier aspects of his patients' wounds. His job would be to inspire the patients to find themselves, to believe in it, to seek it, and to find it. It—and not any doctor—would heal their ailments.

A few minutes after Ginley finds it, Zack strides back on stage to find out who has gotten it. Perched in the director's chair, he says, "I want to learn if you know what it is, if you've been able to let go of it and just be it. Some volunteers need to come on stage and tell me what it is." A petite woman with a suntan and dark hair approaches the small staircase leading to the platform. Zack drops from his chair, walks over to the stairs, and says, "You're being brave. Come up with me, and we'll find out what it is." He takes her by the hand and leads her up onto the platform. One of the female helpers runs over quickly and attaches a small microphone to the woman's blouse.

Zack then asks the woman to introduce herself. With her

eyes furtively scanning the room, the woman says that her name is Wendy. Zack says, "Let's have a round of applause for Wendy. She's a miserable cur, but she's going to find out what it is." He then tells Wendy to stand about three feet from him and to look directly into his eyes. He pushes his four-hundred-dollar sunglasses back onto the top of his head; then he puts his hands on her shoulders and peers into her pupils: "Tell me what it is."

"I'm not very good with money," she says.

"I figured that. You're a materialist. Aren't you?"

"Yes, I spend too much money on things that I don't need."

"Yes, I could tell that you're a spendthrift. You're probably very deeply in debt, aren't you?"

Her lower lip begins to tremble. "Yes, I am."

"Tell us how much, Wendy."

"About seven thousand dollars."

"Well, Wendy, tell us all how you got into this mess. Let it go."

Wendy looks sheepish because she has just revealed her financial inadequacies in front of several hundred people. She's hesitates for a minute, and then half asks and half says, "Because I'm really a selfish person?"

Zack smiles and says, "That's right, Wendy. You're really selfish. You're a pig. Let it go. If you let it go, you can find it. And to help you find it, you might want to buy my cassette tape that deals with this very matter: 'How to find it financially.' It's only $25.95. That's just the first step on the road to finding it. (For a quick review of the Five-Step Formula for Getting IT!, see *Table Six*.) You'll have to come back here to The Formula every week and keep working on it until you get it. Getting it is difficult, but I know you can do it, even though you're a selfish pig. At least you know what you are. Don't you?" Wendy is sad to discover that she's so porcine, but she nods timidly.

Table Six: The Five-Step Formula for Getting IT!®

Step 1	Find IT!®
Step 2	Throw IT Away!®
Step 3	Live IT!®
Step 4	Be IT!®
Step 5	Charge IT!®

Zack releases her shoulders and says, "Let's have another round of applause for Wendy. She doesn't get it yet. But she's getting close to it. You can get it, too. You just have to realize that the Formula is that there is no formula. Tear it up; throw it away; be it! Coaches, I must go now." Zack is alluding to the seven o'clock flight to Maui that he has to catch. "I want you to just keep doing it. Help your coachees to get it. It'll take lots of work and return trips to The Formula, which, by the way, are fifty dollars each. We accept Master Card and Visa. Talk to your coach about an installment plan that'll help you to get it. So long."

Another large round of applause breaks out. Cheering erupts. Some people begin crying hysterically, claiming, "I've got it. I've got it." In the little room off to the side of the conference area, adding machines rattle as the day's take is counted. An armored truck rumbles up to the building to whisk it away.

Another six hours of Heather's yelling helps to convince Ginley that although he has a long way to go, he'll eventually get it. After he leaves The Formula that day—with glazed eyes and a stomach ache from the yak milk—he goes home and finds his squat mates engaged in a comparison of ear wax. He's tells them that he's going to change his life and dedicate it to helping others change theirs.

A few days after his first trip to The Formula, Ginley gets himself one job waiting tables and another tutoring people for the GED; he needs the extra money to pay for return visits to The Formula. He also gets a haircut and enrolls in the premed program at a local college.

After completing college and med school and failing his boards the first two times, Ginley becomes certified as a specialist in internal medicine. He sets up shop with an herbalist and a practitioner of acupuncture. His practice goes very well. Although several of his patients die because Ginley prescribes only aspirin for ailments such as kidney infections, people flock to him. Patients are always given acupuncture and a complete course of oregano therapy. Most important, they are taught to look for it, to feel it, and to throw it away.

When Ginley isn't treating his own patients, he acts as a life coach for people starting up new companies. One of his newest clients is Martha Goldblatt, who's going through a nasty divorce and thinking about starting a chain of high-end coffee shops.

He also serves as an independent medical examiner for insurance companies at the rate of $2500 a day. One afternoon Ginley gives testimony on behalf of a coal company being sued by a miner who had his arms and legs hacked off during an industrial accident. While on the stand, Ginley turns toward the plaintiff, whose head and trunk are wheeled into court in a red wagon. Ginley says, "Ladies and gentlemen of the jury, this man just doesn't get it." The good doctor then goes on to explain that the miner obviously wasn't in tune with it the day he got hurt. "If he had been with it, he would have had the good sense to get out of the way of the drilling machine. Besides," argues Ginley, "the man can still find it without arms and legs. In fact," continues Ginley, "limbs can just get in its way."

The jury is moved by Ginley's impassioned testimony. It is so moved that it rules that the accident was the man's own fault, simply the spoils of not being "with it." In fact, the miner not only fails to win compensation, he's also fined several thousand dollars, the cost of the company having to shut down the drilling machine while the worker's legs were searched for by his colleagues. After the trial, Ginley compliments the members of the jury for their ability to get it, and he gently reminds Counsel for the Defense of the correct address for the check.

What not to do:

By believing in themselves, Ginley and many others like him have been able to find the strength to overcome obstacles. Believers such as Dr. Ginley discover the courage to do things that should best remain undone. Fortunately, though, you can do something about the destructiveness of belief.

1. Don't go to meetings of spirituality groups.

Most belief systems will collapse if their adherents don't receive pep talks at regular intervals. If you don't want to find yourself going on a Crusade or drinking yak milk, don't attend self-help seminars.

2. Never talk to anyone on the subway or in a public park.

Picture this: You're sitting on the A-Train and a pretty young thang sidles up to you. She says: "My name is Debbie, and I'd like to invite you to come to a really neat party with really cool people." Change seats immediately. If she follows you, try pepper spray. These benign-seeming invitations are often merely a ruse employed by cults to get their hands on you and your wallet. Once you're in their grip you just might find yourself sporting a shaved head and standing at the check-in line at an airport, next to the MPs. There you'll peddle copies of the *Bhagavad-Gita* to college students headed to Cancun for spring break. Or, worse yet, you could be using your new self-esteem to do something truly dreadful, such as writing a winning marketing plan for a new brand of whiskey.

Remember, whenever some stranger approaches you and asks to talk, just say no.

3. Never, ever read self-help manuals.

If you read the story of David and Goliath, for example, you just might find the strength to lead your small Internet start-up company to victory. Your company will enable gun owners to buy pistols from an offshore warehouse. You'll go head-to-head with Smith and Wesson. And armed with your self-esteem, you'll grab a sixty-two percent market share in Saturday Night Specials. People will be walking around the streets armed with your guns, which will have engraved on their grips the text of the twenty-third Psalm. Please do us all a favor and stop reading inspirational literature.

§

Chapter 6:
The Myth of Creativity

Creativity is the key to happiness, some say. Everybody—from the soul-deadened administrative assistant to the predatory corporate raider—aspires to creativity. What exactly do we mean when we term someone 'creative'? At the core of the matter, to be creative is to be possessed of an impulse to make something—usually a mess. We live in an age in which creativity is held as one of the highest ends that we can achieve. If we want to bestow a compliment on a fellow traveler, we wouldn't dream of describing that person as hardworking, crafty, or—even, dare we say it—smart. No, these appellations just won't do for those operating at peak performance. Rather, we say that the person in question is creative. The way the word "creativity" is bandied about these days, one might think that we live in an age of suburban Michelangelos painting away in cul-de-sacs all over the nation.

What most people term creativity is generally limited to the realm of the shrewd endeavor. For example, we call greedy but ambitious corporate executives creative if they pioneer exciting new ways of securing for themselves vice presidencies. Unfortunately, these methods generally involve the employment of cheap overseas sweatshop labor. We also bestow the label of creativity on lawyers who discover technical grounds upon which timorous juries can find corporate scoundrels innocent. And we rave about the creativity of rapacious marketers, who—desperate to pay off the mortgages on their second homes in Bermuda—find new ways of compelling us to buy the same old oatmeal.

Of course, creativity is also a quality that we see as the special province of those who call themselves artists. For roughly one-hundred years, art has been our secular religion. Well, of course, business is really our religion. But most of us can't admit that making money is all that life offers. So we go to galleries filled with awful paintings, attend arty and plotless films featuring voiceovers by Max Von Sydow, and read rather morose novels about army officers wearing pig suits.

Of all the types of art produced, perhaps that with the most profound impact upon our nation is that of the film. Very few of us attend the theater. Less than ten percent of us read serious fiction, but all of us go to the movies. Our fantasy life, rather dreary by most standards, is largely determined by the kinds of movies that we view. Filmmakers, then, help to shape the moviegoer's consciousness. For example, many of us became afraid of ascending skyscrapers after seeing *The Towering Inferno*. After viewing *Jaws*, more of us developed a morbid fear of wading at the beach. And even more of us—bucket-loads, multitudes—wanted to become archeologists or intergalactic swashbucklers after seeing Harrison Ford at work.

The movie. It's not just an entertainment. It is—and has been for three quarters of a century—a way of life.

Thus, filmmakers have become the true spiritual architects and dictators of our time. They command casts of hundreds, crews of thousands, and audiences of millions. They inflict upon viewers their own obsessions and peculiarities. These idiosyncrasies, along with product placements, have been focus-group fine-tuned to appeal the greatest number of people possible. Who are these cultural overlords who exercise such a profound impact on our thoughts?

I'm glad you asked. Let's enroll in NYU's film school and have our own screening of *Saving Private Ryan's Credit Rating*, the M.F.A. project of Frederick P. Zalston. Fred is a budding young writer whose thesis advisor is Stephen Lee, a world-renowned filmmaker. Lee has told Fred that if his project is well written, he just might buy and produce it.

Because Lee believes that good filmmaking is good business, he has encouraged all of his students to make their scripts more likely to get corporate backing. Thus, Lee asserts, the young filmmakers should insert into their scripts commercial themes, as well as placements of products and services produced by companies targeted for sponsorship. When Fred first heard of the corporate shaping of movies, he was scandalized. "I produce art, not dreck. I don't cater to the base whims of a deadened movie-going audience." But after Lee had bought *The Return of Martin Guerre in a Ford Explorer*, which had been written by one of Fred's classmates, Zalston knew that the handwriting was on the wall.

When Zalston had told Lee that he would do a script for a World War II picture, his mentor had been enthusiastic. War movies had been doing quite well. And, Lee had said, NYU would be just the place to write such a script, since the university houses the ***Stephen Ambrose Center for the Sentimentalizing of the Second World War***. Tom Brokaw would even be doing public readings from his series of books about the conflict: *The Greatest Generation* (a compilation of letters home from soldiers), *The Greatest Generation Makes a Nest* (a compilation of letters from former soldiers to their real-estate agents), and *The Greatest Generation Does Dallas* (a compilation of the arrest records of soldiers on leave).

Before beginning his script, Zalston discusses the project with his instructor, who says that he should aim for a story line that will make Americans feel good about the mindless slaughter while delivering to them commercial messages. (For a partial listing of classic movies currently being remade to feature advertisements and product placements, see *Table Seven.*) Armed with this advice and hoping for a sale, Zalston goes to work. The following is the script that he writes and that Lee in fact buys.

Table Seven: Movies Currently Being Remade to Feature Product Placements & Commercial Themes

Original Title	Remake Title
Apocalypse Now	*Be All that You Can Be*
Gone with the Wind	*Ted Turner sets Atlanta on Fire*
Strangers on a Train	*No Strangers on Amtrak*
Mr. Smith Goes to Washington	*Mr. Smith takes the Delta Shuttle to BWI*
Goldfinger	*Goldcard*
Once Upon a Time in the West	*Welcome to Marlboro Country*
Twelve Angry Men	*Twelve Men Doing Better on Prozac*
The Three Musketeers	*The Three Musketeers and Kit Kat*
Dr. Strangelove	*How I Learned to Stop Protesting and Love Lockheed*
Dr. Zhivago	*Dr. Zhivago's Managed Care Practice*

Saving Private Ryan's Credit Rating

By Frederick P. Zalston

In Partial Fulfillment of the Requirements of the Degree of Master of Fine Arts in Film New York University

INT -- DAY -- SENATOR LOTT'S OFFICE

The Office of Iowa Senator Dashall Lott, July 1944. Behind the desk are an American flag and a giant Coca-Cola symbol. The Senator is speaking to an elderly woman who has obviously lived on a farm all her life. The woman, MRS RYAN, holds in her right hand a framed picture of her son dressed in a World War-II-era army uniform. In her left hand she holds a duplicate copy of an American Express bill. The Senator looks both official and sympathetic. Mrs. Ryan is crying.

MRS. RYAN

Senator, I told him not to leave home without it. If he doesn't pay his bill soon, he could get a bad credit rating. My son, part of the greatest generation, is fighting for his country somewhere in France. He's struggling against all odds to make the world safe from Fascism, and now you tell me that there's no way to get this duplicate copy of his bill to him. He only has four days before his credit rating is affected. Senator, it's just not American.

THE SENATOR

(touched by a mother's love for her son)

You're right, ma'am. Part of what this war is about is making sure that all Americans have good credit ratings. Just think what would happen if the Nazis and the Japs took over. They'd have the banks place holds on all of our lines of personal credit. And they'd send trumped-up past-due notices. It would be utter chaos. That can't happen--Thank God--in this wonderful nation of ours. Don't worry, Mrs.

Ryan, we'll make sure that your boy, wherever he is, has the opportunity to pay his bill.

ZOOM IN on the grim determination on the Senator's face, PAN TO the single tear on Mrs. Ryan's cheek, PAN TO the giant Coca-Cola symbol behind the Senator's desk.

CUT TO:

EXT - DAY - WHITE HOUSE

FOLLOW a long black car motoring through war-time Washington. The car finally pulls up in front of the White House.

CUT TO:

INT - DAY - OVAL OFFICE

In the Office are the Senator, President Franklin Roosevelt, and General George Marshall. The President, with his cigarette holder clamped in his mouth, sits behind his desk, calmly listening to the Senator's story about Private Ryan. Behind the President, and to his right, stands at rigid attention General Marshall.

PRESIDENT ROOSEVELT

God damn it, if we win this war and this boy loses his credit rating, none of this will have been worth the effort. When's the final deadline on the notice?

THE SENATOR

He has four days.

PRESIDENT ROOSEVELT

My god, that doesn't give us much time.

Roosevelt turns to General Marshall.

PRESIDENT ROOSEVELT

General, this boy is behind the lines in France. Can you find him for us?

GENERAL MARSHALL

(turning to a map of France)

Absolutely, Mr. President. His unit is near the town of St. Raoul. We'll drop in the 241st Extraction Brigade via parachute and we'll make sure that they take with them a paymaster who can make an advance on Ryan's salary.

PRESIDENT ROOSEVELT
At what percent interest? We want to be damn fair about this.

THE SENATOR
Well, the Prime's at seven right now.

PRESIDENT ROOSEVELT
We'll shave off a point off since he's one of our brave fighting boys.

The Senator appears relieved, but he looks at the bill again, and his eyes go wide.

THE SENATOR
My god, Mr. President.

PRESIDENT ROOSEVELT
Yes, Senator? You look like you've just seen a Republican.

THE SENATOR
This bill says that you can't send cash. All of our effort will be for naught.

The President looks consternated.

PRESIDENT ROOSEVELT
That's a new rub. General, what can we do about this on your end?

GENERAL MARSHALL
It's not a problem, Mr. President. I have a plan.

PRESIDENT ROOSEVELT
(smiling)
I bet you do.

GENERAL MARSHALL
We'll send in a specialist from Western Union. After they find Ryan and the specialist writes out a money order, I'll have the 241st meet up with the Maquis. And then Eighth Air Force will carpet bomb

the area.

THE SENATOR
Won't the bombing kill some of our boys?

GENERAL MARSHALL
Senator, a man's credit rating is at stake here. The future of consumer confidence and the entire post-war economy ride on what we're going to decide in this room. Just imagine what would happen if the Russians found out that one of our heroes got a bad credit rating precisely when he was working to save his capitalist overlords. My god, they would have a field day with it.

PRESIDENT ROOSEVELT
We can't let that happen, General. I won't have the Russians making political hay out of our failure to protect one man's credit rating. General, get Eighth Air Force on the horn and tell them that they have carte blanche to lay waste to everything once we find our man.

General Marshall hesitates for a moment.

GENERAL MARSHALL
Sir, what about the St. Raoul Coca-Cola bottling plant?

THE SENATOR
Good Lord, I own twenty-thousand shares of Coke. We can't bomb that plant.

PRESIDENT ROOSEVELT
All right, Senator. Rest assured that your commander-in-chief won't let the value of your investment plummet. What you're about to hear can never leave this room. General, get the hotline out. It's a matter of corporate survival.

THE SENATOR
Hotline? What hotline, Mr. President?

The General opens up a cabinet behind the President's desk. Inside is a red phone under a glass cake cover. On the phone is an AT&T globe symbol. The General removes the cake cover and presses a button on the phone. At first there's silence. Then the General says a few words in German, and he hands the phone to President Roosevelt.

GENERAL MARSHALL
He'll be on the line in just a minute, sir.

PRESIDENT ROOSEVELT
Very good, General. Gentlemen, I think I'm going to need a little liquid refreshment. If you'd be so kind.

The President points to a wet bar near the door to the Oval Office. The General and the Senator go over to the bar and begin to mix the President a rum-and-Coke. A moment of silence ensues, and then the President's expression changes.

PRESIDENT ROOSEVELT
Dolph, how are you, old boy?

THE SENATOR
(to General Marshall)
My god, is that Adolph Hitler?

GENERAL MARSHALL
Yes, we have direct lines to the heads of state of all the Axis powers.

THE SENATOR
Why would we want that? We're at war with them.

GENERAL MARSHALL
Very true, but sometimes business must take priority over pleasure.

PRESIDENT ROOSEVELT
Yes, Dolph, I'm sorry about those pill boxes. Yes, I know that they're expensive. But what about all that shipping your U-boat boys blew up a couple of years ago? That wasn't very nice either. Yeah, I know. It was mostly razor blades and ice boxes. But Gillette was really ticked off. You know that we marked the ships that were carrying munitions. I can't help it if your periscopes aren't very good.

Look, Dolph, I've got some inside information about a little carpet bombing that the boys at Eighth Air Force are going to be doing this week. I can't help your troops. You know the rules. But what I can do is to let you know that the St. Raoul Coke bottling plant is inside the area of the carpet bombing. What do you mean that you don't have any anti-aircraft guns left? I thought old Albert Speer was just cranking out munitions for your boys.

President Roosevelt is grinning widely.

GENERAL MARSHALL
(to the Senator)
He likes goading Hitler about their underproduction.

PRESIDENT ROOSEVELT
Dolph, how many shares of Coca-Cola does the Reich own? Hmm. That's about what I thought. Look, the Gestapo pension funds can't be doing too well right now. Yes, yes, I know. You have all those secret weapons. Are they going to be as big of a hit as that heavy water stuff was?

The President giggles.

PRESIDENT ROOSEVELT
Look, Dolph, don't get mad at me just because I happen to run the Arsenal of Democracy. I'm doing you a favor. No, no, Dolph. I don't know about anything going on at Los Alamos. Let's get back on the subject. I'll do my best to have my boys avoid collateral damage, but if you want your pension funds to do well, I'd advise you to move your heavy anti-aircraft guns to the plant area. You really don't have any?

The President covers up the telephone for a second.

PRESIDENT ROOSEVELT
(to the Senator and General Marshall)
Hee, hee, the boys at Eighth Air Force are doing better than I thought they were.

The President uncovers the speaker.

PRESIDENT ROOSEVELT
Hang on a second, Dolph.
The President motions for General Marshall to come over. Marshall hands Roosevelt a drink.

GENERAL MARSHALL
Yes, Mr. President?

PRESIDENT ROOSEVELT
General, can we drop about twenty or thirty gliders in near the plant area? We need to get some protection in to those boys.

GENERAL MARSHALL
I'll call Transport Command immediately, sir. We'll have those guns in there right away.

The Senator looks shocked.

THE SENATOR
We're giving anti-aircraft guns to the Germans?

The President glowers at the Senator.

PRESIDENT ROOSEVELT
Do you want to send your kid to Yale or not? Coca-Cola is blue chip. We have to think about the bigger economic picture and not get bogged down in details. Here, have a Coke and a smile.

The President hands the Senator a bottle of Coca-Cola. The Senator thinks for a moment and breaks into a grin.

THE SENATOR
What's good for the soft-drink bottling industry is good for America.

PRESIDENT ROOSEVELT
That's what I like to hear, Senator. Play your cards right, and you just might have a place at the United Nations after the war.

"I'd like to buy the World a Coke" begins to play softly in the background. A loud and angry German-speaking voice erupts from the phone.

PRESIDENT ROOSEVELT

One moment, gentlemen. Sorry, Dolph, I was just sharing a Coke with some friends. Tell your boys that they'll be getting some anti-aircraft guns tomorrow night. Try not to shoot down any of the gliders, Dolph. Yeah, yeah, I know. Luftwaffe pilots never hit the wrong target. What's this? I suppose I can do that. Let's say at ten dollars a crate? Done. I have to go. Give my best to Eva and Blondi. What's that? No, Dolph, I can't do anything about the Berlin raids. They're your problem. Look, I have Tojo on Line Two.

The President hangs up the phone and smiles at the Senator and General Marshall.

PRESIDENT ROOSEVELT

I just love ribbing him. Tojo always puts him on hold.

THE SENATOR

What did Hitler want at the end?

PRESIDENT ROOSEVELT

Nylons, Senator. Those German boys may be great soldiers, but they're not so good at manufacturing synthetic fabrics.

The President holds up a Leggs container.

PRESIDENT ROOSEVELT

Gentlemen, we've done a great deal toward establishing the post-war consumer economy this morning. We've set plans in motion to save the credit rating of one of our gallant heroes of democracy, and we've worked to preserve the assets of one of the cornerstones of that new economy. We should be proud.

At that moment an AIDE runs in to the Oval Office.

AIDE

Mr. President, we've just found out that the Japanese have captured Lord Montbatten's supply of Absolut.

The President shakes his head slowly.

PRESIDENT ROOSEVELT

Those little Nips. Will they never learn? General, get Carl Spatz on the line. Tell him to bomb the hell out of the first Toyota factory that we can find.

The light begins to soften. The President bends over his table of important notes. The General is on the phone. And the Senator is drinking a bottle of Coke. The Coke theme plays in the background. The President, the Senator, and the General all sway in time to the music.

FADE OUT.

EXT - NIGHT - C-47

WE SEE five transports carrying the 241st Extraction Brigade. Each of the planes drags behind it an advertising banner. ZOOM IN ON BANNER 1 "Drink Ovaltine." BANNER 2 - "Winston tastes good, like a cigarette should." BANNER 3, "If you had flown American, you'd be bayoneting a Kraut by now." BANNER 4, "Apple--Think Different." BANNER 5 sports a picture of Chiang Kai-Shek wearing a World War II-era bomber jacket made by Members Only.

CUT TO:

INT - NIGHT - C-47

The interior of a C-47, 4 AM. Approximately thirty-five men are sitting against the walls of the plane. All are quiet. WE SEE FOUR YOUNG MEN - the intrepid and customer-friendly captain, BILL KROC, the older brother of McDonald's founder Ray Kroc. To his right sits Corporal LEE IACOCCA, an Italian-Japanese American, looking sharp in his crisp WESTERN UNION uniform. To his left sits Lieutenant WILLIE GATES, who is Cherokee. Cheerful banter begins.

LIEUTENANT GATES

Cap, these Happy Meals are a great idea: tiny burgers and an order of french fries. They're just what I need before I parachute into enemy territory.

CAPTAIN KROC

Yeah, I don't know what inspired me, but the beauty of the Happy Meal is that each of the components is utterly interchangeable and replaceable.

UNSEEN SOLDIER
Yeah, just like us.

Laughter comes from the rest of the crew members.

CAPTAIN KROC
Well, I guess we are all replaceable, Nivens. But that's what makes us different from the Krauts. They see themselves as being special, unique. That's why they have all that master-race stuff. But we Americans know that we're all pretty much alike. Every Taylorist man jack of us, we're just cogs in the wheel of democratic but non-unionized capitalism. We're standardized parts that make the machine run smoothly. You won't see any of us claim to be geniuses. No, sir. America's a big place, but it's filled with small people, people happy with their own smallness.

CORPORAL IACOCCA
You know, this war has given us a chance to forget about our own problems and to focus in on quality, which is Job One.

LIEUTENANT GATES
You said it, Corp. That's what this war is all about. Quality, Choice, and Service. I spent a year studying in Germany back in 1937, and the customer service at restaurants was really terrible. Yeah, the consumer goods were well made, but there wasn't much choice. And things lasted forever. How can you claim to be the master race when you don't even have planned obsolescence? The Krauts are pretty good at speculative philosophy, romantic literature, and bombastic opera, but when you get right down to it, they're really shitty at marketing to the consumer. And that lack of commitment to excellence is going to cost them this war.

The Lieutenant's voice has been rising. At that moment, the squadron of planes crosses over into enemy territory, and a flak barrage begins. The camera shows the five planes flying in a standard Nike Swoosh Formation. Little puffs of black smoke begin to erupt. One of the planes is engulfed in flames. From the soldiers in Captain Kroc's plane come epithets and shouts of horror. Captain Kroc gets onto the intercom, which connects him to the soldiers in all four surviving planes.

CAPTAIN KROC

Gentlemen, no one ever promised us a rose garden. Yes, we have to break some eggs to make an omelette. But if we just put our shoulders to the wheel and our noses to the grindstone, we can win one for the gipper. We've fought some hard battles before. There was our rescue of the two Ford executives from Corregidor back in '42. That was tough. But our work in the Pacific enabled the assembly lines of democracy to continue to churn out inferior-quality tanks. Then there was our saving of Captain Jenkins, the Madison Avenue executive who is now writing incredible recruiting ads. But gentlemen, all of our past work pales in comparison with our mission now. This time, boys, we're saving the credit rating of one of our fighting men. The President himself has sent us on this mission, because he knows that good credit ratings are essential to success in the post-war consumer economy that we're all going to enjoy. We have it in our power to get the late charges removed from a man's bill. Very few human beings have ever been similarly empowered in any war. So Hannibal crossed the Alps. So Washington snuck up on a few napping Hessians. So Sherman turned Atlanta into a smoking ash heap. Did any of these military leaders ever save a man's credit rating? No, gentlemen, none ever did. And that's what makes our army and our war different. We're fighting for the right of the common man to spend freely and get himself into barely manageable debt. Some of us won't make it back from this mission. But we'll die knowing that we've made the world a little bit better for consumers. Boys, in addition to your Happy Meals, you've each been issued a special package sent directly from the President. I'd like you to open it now.

The camera pans through each of the four planes and shows men ripping open sealed cardboard boxes. Inside each of the boxes is a bottle of Coke to which is affixed the Presidential seal.

CAPTAIN KROC

Gentlemen, on behalf of the President of the United States, I invite you to have a Coke and a smile.

The soldiers, dressed in full combat gear and wearing both front- and back-mounted parachutes, take off the lids of the Coke bottles with church keys. ZOOM IN on bottle opener -- emblazoned with "Drive across the post-War USA in your heavily financed Chevrolet."
Each soldier takes a long swallow and turns to his fellows, with a look of refreshment on his face.
The youngest soldier, THE KID, who has red hair and freckles, starts singing, "I'd like to buy the world a Coke." Corporal Iacocca jumps in, singing, "And keep it company." The rest of the soldiers begin to sing, swaying back-and-forth in time to the music.
After two verses, the soldiers' voices are replaced by those of the MORMON TABERNACLE CHOIR.
ZOOM IN on the red and green signal lights over the hatch. The red light blinks out, and the green one becomes illuminated. Corporal Iacocca jumps up and opens the door.
Outside the plane, flak continues to erupt. All of the soldiers stand up and click the static lines of their parachutes onto the wire above their heads.
The singing of the Coke song increases in volume.
Each soldier has a Thompson sub-machine gun in his left hand and a bottle of Coke in his right. The lines of soldiers reach the doors. As each soldier in the lead plane approaches the open door, the Captain pats him on the shoulder and pushes him out.
The Coke theme gets louder.

CUT TO:

EXT - NIGHT - PLANES

Spotlights from the ground shine up on the descending paratroopers, who are drinking their Cokes and firing their Thompsons at the German machine-gun emplacements. Tracers streak into the sky. As some of the paratroopers are killed, their machine guns fall to the ground. But their Coke bottles hang from their necks by lanyards. The planes have begun to pull up and turn toward the

Channel. One plane is hit. Its right engine bursts into flame.
ZOOM IN on the look of terror on the face of the young pilot, who's desperately trying to pull the nose up. His copilot is dead and flopped over the controls. His Coke bottle is clutched tightly in his right hand. As the plane begins to plummet, the camera focuses on the fuselage, on which are painted five Pepsi bottles. Each bottle has a giant "X" through it. The plane continues its descent, and its engines begin to whine. An explosion is heard coming from out of camera range.
ZOOM IN on the face of the Kid who began the Coke song. Wearing a determined expression on his face, the Kid fires his Thompson wildly and takes deep gulps of Coke. Suddenly, he's caught in the glare of a spotlight. Tracers fly upward and tear into him and his field pack. The camera focuses for a moment on the pack, out of which falls the Kid's Happy Meal.
The Meal lands on the lap of a German soldier manning an American anti-aircraft gun. He opens the box and takes out a french fry. Just as the soldier is about to eat the fry, he's ripped apart by bullets coming from two Thompsons. BACK TO Lieutenant Gates and Corporal Iacocca, who nod to each other grimly as the German soldier dissolves into an anatomically correct pile of flesh and bone.
ZOOM IN on the Kid again. He grimaces and looks toward the Captain, who is one parachute over.
The Kid lets his machine gun drop. But he takes a final slug of Coke and makes a thumbs-up sign. With tears welling up in his eyes, the Captain lets his Thompson hang by its strap. He also takes a slug of Coke and locks eyes with the Kid. The Captain returns the Kid's thumbs-up sign. The Kid smiles for a second, with blood and Coke coming out of the corner of his mouth, then slumps lifelessly in his harness. The Captain frowns and then drops a grenade into a machine-gun emplacement. There's a wild explosion, and eight German bodies are thrown into the air. The camera focuses on the severed arm of one of the German soldiers. Tightly clenched in the hand is a bottle of "Deutschland Cola."
WIDE ANGLE of the Brigade descending. All are drinking Coke and firing Thompsons. Another transport

bursts into flame. The volume at which the Mormon Tabernacle Choir continues loudly humming the Coke theme increases.

FADE OUT

EXT - NIGHT - SHELL CRATER

A shell crater ten yards across and two miles from the drop zone, about twenty minutes before the arrival of the 241st Extraction Brigade. It's a very light night. Four Americans are crouching in the hole. Each looks outward, keeping a sharp watch and occasionally ducking his head after hearing the crack of a shot fired by one of several German snipers who surround the crater.
Each wears a tattered uniform. One has a bandage wrapped around his arm. All the soldiers look exhausted and have bags under their eyes. The four soldiers are PRIVATE RYAN and the Sullivan Triplets: SERGEANT FRED, CORPORAL FERD, and PRIVATE VERN. The men are discussing what they will do after the war.

FRED

Me, I think I'll go into Human Resources Management. I really like giving aptitude assessments and personality exams.

FERD

Yeah, that's nice. Me, I want to be a Quality Assurance Supervisor at my local GM Plant. I want to help the common fighting man, Joes like us, to drive the best and safest cars imaginable. I expect that this concern with excellence makes us different from the Nips and the Krauts.

RYAN

What about the Reds?

FERD

Well, Lenin borrowed most of his technology from the Americans Ford and Taylor back in the twenties. The results of Scientific Management and Fordist assembly lines are impressive. But while the Soviets were pretty good at adapting to the contingencies presented by "The Great Leap Forward," they never really found a way to satisfy the needs of the individual consumer. Just compare

GUM with Wanamaker's, for example. Their selection simply isn't as good as ours. Now, of course, the Ruskies have universal health care and are making big strides in recognizing the rights of women and ethnic minorities. And they're in the process of abolishing the shibboleths of organized religion. I'll give them credit where credit is due. But none of their social advances really holds a candle to the pleasure that a man gets when he drives across the post-War USA in his heavily financed Chevrolet.

RYAN

Where did you learn all of that?

FERD

Why, right here in my Penguin Fighting Man Edition of The World Economy at Mid-Century. As you can see, Fighting Man Editions are sized to fit in the leg pocket of your combat pants, right next to your morphine ampoule and suicide capsule. And, best of all, each volume in the Fighting Man Series - elegantly bound in imitation Moroccan leather - is thick enough to stop a fifty-caliber slug. Aesthetics and functionality. That's a war-winning combination, boys. Leni Reifenstal doesn't have anything on us.

At that moment, a grenade sails in over their heads and lands right in the middle of the shell crater.

FRED

Potato masher! Everybody down.

Vern takes off his helmet, throws it on top of the grenade, and belly flops onto the helmet. Ryan and the other two triplets cringe. ZOOM in rapid succession on the faces of the four men.
RYAN's face: surprise and shock.
FRED's face: terror.
FERD's face: constipation.
FLASH BACK to Ferd forgetting to mix Metamucil into his C-Rations that morning. Quick camera placement shot of the "Battle Edition of Metamucil" bottle. On the bottle is the following logo: "Metamucil: Doing its part to win the war, one regular guy at a time."
VERN's face: determination. His eyes are tightly

shut.

VERN

This is it, boys. I guess I'll never get a chance to drive across the post-War USA in my heavily financed Chevrolet. The APR was so sweet. It couldn't be beat. Win one for the gipper.

The seconds crawl by. Nothing happens. Vern opens his eyes and displays a look of pleased surprise. He gets up, picks up the helmet, and looks at the grenade.

VERN

By god, boys, it's a dud.

FERD

See, this shoddy performance is the result of improper management oversight. If the boys at the Krupps factory in Berlin had been employing Quality Assurance Supervisors, this little baby would have done its job and eviscerated my brother here.

FRED

Well, let's show these damned Krauts just what high-quality American-made goods can do.

He takes a grenade from his belt, pulls the pin, and heaves the grenade into the darkness. Two seconds go by. A huge explosion rips through a hedgerow, and the helmeted head of a German soldier lands in the crater.

FRED

See, no duds coming out of the Arsenal of Democracy. Performance and Customer satisfaction, they're going to win this war. And if the grenade hadn't detonated, we could have just radioed into the Help Line at HQ.

Fred picks up the head and holds it level to his own. He looks into the closed eyes.

FRED

Now, Jerry, if you boys had been using Quality

Assurance Supervisors, you'd be holding my head right now. Silly Jerry, duds are for Krauts.

RYAN

Hey, Fred. I'm really tense. Do you still have your hip flask? I could use a shot right now.
Fred reaches into the inside pocket of his fatigue jacket and brings out a flask. Ryan grabs hold of it and takes a long swig.

FRED

Hey, easy there, Ryan. Alcoholic beverages are meant to be enjoyed responsibly. You shouldn't use booze as a crutch for your emotional problems.

RYAN

You mean like a morbid fear of dying horribly in a pool of my own blood and feces while watching my internal organs slither out of a gaping belly wound?

VERN

Look, Ryan, everybody gets a little blue now and then. Mental health problems are nothing to ashamed of. When we get back to base, why don't you make an appointment with Dr. Simmons, the unit psychiatrist? Can you promise me you'll do that? I care about you.

RYAN

Sure, I appreciate your validation of my emotions.

The four men share a group hug.

FERD

Ryan, I bet you didn't know that I'm platoon alcohol-awareness non-commissioned officer this month.

RYAN

No, I didn't.

FERD

While we have a minute between fanatical assaults by Nazi Supermen, let me show you something.

Ferd reaches into his jacket and pulls out a rolled-up piece of cloth about the size of a handkerchief. He unrolls it. On it is embroidered a picture of a human liver.

FERD

Ryan, this is your liver.

Ferd reaches into his pocket and pulls out another piece of cloth and unfurls it. On this piece is also embroidered a picture of a liver. A giant hole is in the liver's center.

FERD

Ryan, this is your liver on alcohol. Get the picture?

At that moment, the transport planes carrying the 241st Extraction Brigade roar overhead, and paratroopers begin to drop down. All men in the crater wave.

FERD

By god, those are our boys. Maybe they've come to help us. Let's pour it on.

All four men begin to fire.

FADE OUT

EXT - DAY - FIELD

WIDE SHOT - ESTABLISH. Half of the members of the 241st Extraction Brigade are dead. The surviving troopers have fought their way through heavy German resistance to a field where they have made contact with agents of the Maquis. Together, the Maquis and the troopers have begun to lay out the signal for the planes that will pick up the team and Private Ryan's paid bill. The symbol is a giant middle finger pointing toward Berlin.

Captain Kroc, Lieutenant Gates, and Corporal Iacocca hide behind the shrubs. Lieutenant Gates begins to stand up, but Ferd, seeing a helmet in the gloom, fires. The bullet ricochets off Lieutenant Gates's helmet.

LIEUTENANT GATES

Jesus Christ, we're the fucking good guys. It says so right here in the script.

He pulls out a copy of Saving Private Ryan's Credit Rating.

LIEUTENANT GATES

See, right here, on page four, it expressly says that we're on the side of the good, the right, and the post-war consumer economy. My character is a combination of John Wayne in The Sands of Iwo Jima and Donald Sutherland in Kelly's Heroes, with a dash of Paul Newman in Cool Hand Luke. What we have here is a failure to communicate.

CAPTAIN KROC

Easy does it, buddy. I'll take care of it.
(shouts toward the crater.)
Hey, you guys! We're the fucking cavalry coming to save Private Ryan's credit rating.

RYAN

Jesus, they know who I am. They have to be Americans.

FERD

Not so fast. Those Germans are pretty tricky. A lot of them speak perfect English. And they could have called a credit bureau. Let's do this by the numbers. (Shouting to Captain Kroc:) Okay, you guys, if you really are Americans and not Kraut bastards, you're going to know the password.

CAPTAIN KROC

Right. The sign is "I'd like to buy the world a Coke." I'd like the countersign.

FERD

"And keep it company."
Smiles on the faces of the rescuers and the men in the crater congratulating each other.

FERD

Okay, come on over. We'll keep you covered.
With the men in the crater laying down covering fire, the rescuers leap into the shell hole. All shake hands. The rescuers distribute spare Cokes and Happy Meals.

CAPTAIN KROC
Is one of you Private Ryan?

RYAN
I am, sir.

CAPTAIN KROC
Thank god. Son, we've come a long way to give you this.

He hands Ryan a duplicate copy of his American Express bill.

RYAN
My god, where did you get that?

CAPTAIN KROC
From your mother. She always has you in her heart. Keep her in yours by sending a Hallmark card next Mother's Day.

Each man has a sweet smile on his face as he thinks of his own beloved mother.

RYAN
Mom, is she okay?

CAPTAIN
She's fine, son. But she's worried about your credit rating. That's why we're here. You forgot to pay your last bill, and you're almost sixty days past due. The resulting bad credit rating could interfere with your ability to buy a Levittown-style tract home after the war.

RYAN
Well, I didn't forget. I just thought I wouldn't pay. It's only about thirty dollars. It's not that big of a deal.

LIEUTENANT GATES
(explodes with rage)
Not that big of a deal? Ryan, do you know how many good men, good consumers, have died in order for us to get this duplicate bill to you? My god, if you don't give a shit about your own credit rating,

think about the sacrifices all these men have made. Be a fucking man.

CAPTAIN KROC

Easy, Willie. We're all on the same Quality Assurance Team here.

He takes Ryan by a shoulder and leads him over to the edge of the crater.

CAPTAIN KROC

Son, I hate to do this. I'm about to lay a very heavy weight on you, but I think you're man enough to take it. Ryan, have you thought very much about what the world will look like after we get through kicking German ass?

RYAN

No, Captain. I just always sort of thought that things would go back to being pretty much like they were before Pearl. Slipping back into Isolationism, never getting much past second base with my girlfriend because of a lack of reliable prophylactics, and receiving fairly generous subsidies from a variety of New Deal agencies.

At that moment, a German soldier carrying a bayonet runs maniacally toward the shell hole. Captain Kroc lights a cigarette with one hand and shoots the German with a forty-five that he holds in the other. The German's body pitches forward, and his bloody head lands on one of the Captain's well-polished boots.

CAPTAIN KROC

(muttering to himself)

Damn, I just had that boot shined last night.

(To Ryan)

Cigarette, son?

RYAN

What kind, Captain?

CAPTAIN KROC

It's a Winston. It tastes good, like a cigarette should.

Ryan takes a cigarette, and the Captain lights it for him. At the same time the Captain shoots another German who is running toward the hole.

CAPTAIN KROC

Ryan, things aren't going to be like they were. I guess we Americans have lost our innocence in this war. But we've gained a whole lot more. When we begin to produce butter in addition to guns, we'll be doing it with a whole different kind of industrial plant. And we won't make just butter, either. We'll have an incredible variety of consumer goods, so we'll need people to be able to get into just barely manageable debt. We'll need people who can meet their minimum monthly payments.

RYAN

And that's where I come in?

CAPTAIN KROC

Yeah, Ryan, that's where you come in. That's why we've brought your bill.

RYAN

I can't believe that I'm worth the effort.

CAPTAIN KROC

Frankly, Ryan, you're not. You're a symbol, one that we have to protect. Here you are, fighting for your country, for GM, Chrysler, and Coca-Cola. We can't let you die without giving you a chance to leave your credit rating in good order. It would make your government look bad, and it might cause a downturn in consumer confidence. Think about it, Ryan. Very few men have the opportunity to make an impact on an entire civilization's credit worthiness. Now, you don't have to pay your bill. You can just let it lapse and then get yourself bayonetted, but, hell, Ryan, is that what this man's army is really about?

RYAN

Now that you put it that way, Cap, I'll pay.

CAPTAIN KROC

That-a-boy, Ryan.

At that moment, Corporal Iacocca, who has been rereading the bill, interjects.

CORPORAL IACOCCA
Skipper, we've got a problem.

CAPTAIN KROC
What, no room for the planes to land?

CORPORAL IACOCCA
Nah, Cap. The strip will be just fine.

Two C-47s roar in low over the trees. The transports are accompanied by twenty fighter planes. Peeling out of their Nike Swoosh Formation, they begin to strafe the area near the shell hole. High overhead can be seen hundreds of B-17 bombers. ZOOM IN ON BOMBER PILOT.

PILOT
Attention all planes; stand-by to begin Operation Consumer Confidence. Bomb-bay doors open.

BACK TO the shell crater.

CAPTAIN KROC
Well, what's the problem, Iacocca?

CORPORAL IACOCCA
Cap, I've been reading the fine print on the duplicate bill. Even if he gives us the money order to bring back, the payment is so late that it'll have to be made in person at a branch office.

CAPTAIN KROC
Good work, Iacocca. Ryan, it looks like you're going home, son.

Heavy fire begins. Lieutenant Gates is killed. All in the shell crater begin to return the German fire.

CORPORAL IACOCCA
Cap, we've got to go now.

CAPTAIN KROC
Iacocca, you take Ryan and the triplets. I'll hold

the Krauts off for as long as I can.

CORPORAL IACOCCA
Skipper, it's suicide.

The triplets have been talking among themselves.

FERD
Captain Kroc, we want to do our part for the consumer economy. We're staying. Ryan, good luck.

Ryan looks thankful. He and Iacocca crawl out of the shell hole and run to the landing field. The heavy bombing begins. The first planeload of commandos takes off. The second transport begins to taxi. Ryan and Iacocca run alongside the plane. Ryan is pulled in. He grabs Iacocca's hand, in which the American Express bill is held. A hole appears in the Corporal's helmet. Iacocca pulls his hand away and falls to the ground. Ryan is left holding the duplicate bill as the plane lifts off.

CUT TO:

EXT - DAY - SHELL CRATER

Hundreds of Germans are over-running the crater in slow motion. In order of ascending rank, each of the triplets is killed. ZOOM IN on their dying faces. Only Captain Kroc is left alive. Wounded in fourteen places, he is out of bullets, grenades, and spit.

In slow motion, he falls backwards. The last shot of him shows him sprawled on his back, with his arms spread out in Christ-like fashion. In his left hand is a Coke. And on his dying face is a smile. The camera shows the plane climbing into the sun and then turning to head back to the white, white cliffs of Dover. The Mormon Tabernacle Choir begins humming the Coke song in a slow, dirge-like manner.

FADE TO BLACK.

EXT - DAY - CEMETERY

The American Military Cemetery in France in 1994. PAN across a crystal blue sky. The Thunderbirds fly overhead in Nike Swoosh Formation.

An aged Private Ryan, dressed in a natty Members Only jacket, and accompanied by his wife and children, as well as his grandchildren, is walking through the cemetery. All are drinking Cokes. And the children are carrying Saving Private Ryan's Credit Rating tie-in Happy Meals. In the background can be seen the American flag, as well as flags bearing the corporate symbols and logos for Microsoft, Mary-Kay, McDonald's, Ford, and, of course, Coca-Cola. RYAN'S SON, a well dressed man in his mid-forties, yells to his father.

RYAN'S SON
Dad, I think we've found it!

Ryan shambles over to the grave around which the rest of the family is gathered.

RYAN
My god, there it is.

Ryan has a tear in his eye. ZOOM IN on the gravestone: "Captain Bill Kroc, brother of the founder of McDonald's and originator of The Happy Meal."

RYAN
Every time I turn on my VCR or get my American Express Bill, I think of the Captain and what I owe him, what we in the post-war consumer-oriented economy owe him.

The Coca-Cola song is sung one final time by the Mormon Tabernacle Choir. The camera pans slowly over all the corporate logos fluttering in the breeze

FADE TO CREDITS AND CORPORATE SPONSORS

What not to do.

There you have it. One person strove to be creative. And he succeeded in engulfing the rest of us in a miasma of sentimentality and consumerism. What can you do to guarantee that you don't follow in the path of Frederick P. Zalston? I'm glad you asked. There are some simple steps that you can not take.

1. Don't indulge your whimsy.

If you think you have a great idea, forget about it. Don't let your imagination wander. It just might arrive at the outlands of *Gone with the Wind* or *Battlestar Galactica.* Remember, in this day and age, your imagination—if well-financed—just might oppress the hell out of me. How many of us can hear the William Tell Overture without thinking of the Lone Ranger? How many of us can think of New York's nickname without also thinking of the Caped Crusader? Don't colonize anybody else's imagination, and don't develop your own.

2. Don't develop your talents.

Even if you ignore the above advice, there's still a great deal of hope left. The most impressive talents can't be developed without a great deal of painstaking effort and years of practice. So, don't take any drawing classes. Don't enroll in any writing workshops. Don't go to open-mike nights. If we're all lucky, your ideas will amount to absolutely nothing and cause the rest of us absolutely no harm.

3. Don't read, see movies, or go to exhibitions.

People learn by imitation. What we see often helps us to develop our own ideas. So, the less we see, read, or hear, the less chance we have of expressing what's in our heads and hearts. And, generally, this is a good state of affairs. Think about how different our own imaginations would be if we hadn't grown up watching *Jaws*, *Gilligan's Island*, and *Star Trek*. All of the writers of these pieces of entertainment developed their own ideas by reading, watching, and listening to the works of other artists. For god's sake, close your eyes and stopper your ears.

§

Chapter 7:

The Myth of Self-Denial

The literary scholar Camille Paglia has said that much of what we call great in Western culture owes its existence to sublimated male sexual energy. Of course it's wonderful that the pent-up orgasm has produced the *Mona Lisa*, the Rumba, and *The Great Gatsby*. Unfortunately, it's also responsible for the Inquisition, the Battle of the Somme, and *Gilligan's Island.* Acting in the spirit of the financial times (and *The Wall Street Journal*), we should perform a cost-benefit analysis of a case study in order to determine exactly what self-denial does for us.

Most of us are familiar with Bram Stoker's novel about that quite revolting creature, Count Dracula. Most people also know that Stoker's creation was based on a true-life figure named Vlad Dracul, a minor noble in the fifteenth-century. But although many readers are somewhat familiar with the tale of he who hates garlic, the full story doesn't appear in history textbooks. So let's return to those thrilling days of the Middle Ages and see the way in which the practice of self-denial almost destroyed the career of our favorite vampire.

Welcome to the kingdom of Wallachia on Wednesday, December 13, 1448. It's been a bad day. Those pesky Turks have just paid a visit to Tirgoviste, slaughtering over fifty residents and carrying away another dozen, including Mrs. Romanovsky, the town's favorite gypsy fortuneteller. The local branch of the Wallachian Chamber of Commerce is scandalized. Georg von Blechstein, the Chamber's president, addresses a hastily convened meeting of the executive committee: "These raids by the Turks are a disaster. Our economy is going to be devastated, and we won't be able to qualify for matching grant money from the IMF for that convention center and self-flagellation house."

"We have to do something. The situation is getting out of

hand," agrees Andre Cordinski. Andre's appearance is a little askew because of the arrow sticking out of his chest. The proprietor of a local bed and breakfast, Andre says, "Look, I don't mind the raids. They're just politics. And at least the Turks don't smell as bad as the Mongols, with their damned shaggy ponies. But these Ottomans aren't even patronizing local businesses. They just plunder us and then stay at the Constantinople Holiday Inn. Somebody has to lay down the law here. The Turks simply must reinvest their hard-plundered booty."

Julian Lubinski, owner of a livery stable, turns toward the head of the table and asks, "Georg, have you gone up to the castle and requested help?"

Georg shakes his head slowly. "Things just haven't been the same since the old king died. He would have been able to handle this situation quite nicely. We wouldn't be in the tight spot that we're in now if he were still alive." Georg is wistfully referring to the recently deceased ruler of Wallachia, Vlad II, nicknamed "Vlad the Destroyer." In his prime, old Vlad had been able to kill a hundred Turks in twenty minutes. His motto was, "The only good Turk is a dead Turk." In the days of his rule, the fearsome Ottomans would ride into the Danube Valley, only to be met by a volley of arrows and about eighty of the nastiest warriors in the world. When the Wallachians ran out of ammunition for their bows, they would simply bite the Turks. After two raids were met with such great hostility and large incisors, the Turks became terrified and left Wallachia alone. With the reputation of its battle-proven leader solidly established, the kingdom had prospered. New condominiums—Dracul's Dachas—were built on the Vistula, and a chain of used sword dealerships and cappuccino stands was established.

But six months before the emergency meeting of the Chamber of Commerce, Vlad the Destroyer had died while making love to one of his several concubines. The era of prosperity had definitively ended. When the old king expired, he was replaced by his seventeen-year-old son, Vlad III. The young king quickly proved to be very different from his father, not possessed of any of the elder Vlad's ferocity. When the boy was young, Vlad's mother had decided to send him to school at the monastery at Jarrow, England, to study with a spiritual disciple of the Venerable Bede.

Although he thought that his son would benefit more by learning how to bite Turks in Wallachia, Vlad acquiesced to his wife's wishes. At the monastery, Vlad became adept at both cooking and calligraphy. He also developed into a good biblical scholar, spending several hours each day studying with his master, Brother Ignatius. Over cups of chamomile tea and the Socratic dialogues, the eye-strained priest stressed to Vlad that while chastity was all well and good, a monk had to have a little pleasure, too. Calmly stroking something, said Brother Ignatius, was a great way to release tension that could build up after several hours of praying and fasting. As a way of encouraging his favorite pupil to develop the habit of stroking, Brother Ignatius gave Vlad a cat, which the young heir to the Wallachian throne named Innocent XVIII.

All was going well at the monastery for Vlad. Not only had he developed a reputation for his calligraphy and Quiche Lorraine, he was also the star of the all-Benedictine monastic bridge team, which was giving the Franciscans a run for their filthy lucre. Except for a few incomprehensible visits by the Scots, the years flew by peacefully. Vlad would have been quite happy to spend the rest of his life at Jarrow, but one day he received the fateful letter from his mother announcing the death of the elder Dracul. Bitterly disappointed, Vlad did not want to leave the monastery and return to the land of garlic.

But Brother Ignatius told his student that he shouldn't shirk his responsibilities to the outside world. The monk reassured his disciple that he would always carry the spirit of Jarrow in his heart. "Don't worry, my son. We'll keep in touch through a direct-mail marketing campaign." After a goodbye party at which there was much stroking and petting, Vlad set off via ship on the long trip home. Accompanied only by Innocent XVIII, Vlad was both bored and terrified on the journey. The peasants he met all smelled bad and ate spoiled cheese. And during the ship's stop on the Italian coast, he saw some awful peasants carrying a statue of St. Raoul, a pickpocket who was canonized for leading a crusade to the Holy Land. Finally, after two months of being at sea and journeying through the Carpathians in a donkey cart, he reached home. Let's look in at the family reunion:

In the castle, he is greeted by his mother, Esmeralda, and by his seven-year-old little sister, Rada. Esmeralda hugs her son and says, "Welcome home, dear." She looks at him, still dressed in his robe and carrying his cat in his arms. She sighs, "Maybe it's a good thing that your father isn't here." In his current attire, Vlad doesn't look very threatening. Esmeralda says, "Dear, I chased away all of your father's concubines. I suppose that it's your right to sleep with them if you want. Would you like me to bring some of them back for you?"

Vlad looks panic stricken. "Mother, I am surprised at you. It's a sin against God and the Church to partake of the flesh when you're not married. Even though my father was a sinner, I am different."

Esmeralda looks at the skinny Vlad and his cat. She sighs again. "You certainly are cut from a very different kind of cloth than your father was. But, dear, you shouldn't put him down just because he used to overindulge his passions a little. He was a good husband and a good leader. And he was a great fighter. He put the Turks in their place."

Rada has been listening quietly. Now she chimes in: "Mommy says that the Turks are going to keep coming back now that Father is dead. Will you slaughter them just like he used to?"

Vlad is thunderstruck and made nervous by the mere mention of violence. He begins to stroke Innocent very quickly, almost harshly. The cat meows and jumps out of Vlad's arms. "No, I am most certainly not going to slaughter them. Killing is another crime against God and man. If the Turks come to Wallachia again, I'll invite them into the castle and make dinner for them. Brother Ignatius taught me that the way to a man's heart is through his stomach."

Rada breaks in again: "Father used to say that the way to a man's heart was through his balls and cock."

Vlad blushes at the mention of male anatomy, but he pretends not to hear or to be affected by his sister's brashness: "I can probably reach these Turks through my Quiche Lorraine. I'm sure that if someone is just understanding with them and shows them that they're loved, then they'll become our friends and treat us with the respect that we deserve."

Rada replies, "Father said the only thing that he didn't understand about the Turks was why someone hadn't slaughtered them a long time ago."

Vlad bends down on one knee so that he can address his little sister at eye level. He says, "Father's gone. I'm in charge now. We won't deal with those we don't like by slaughtering them. Rather, we will express our caring and affection. We'll caress them with our love."

"Caress the Turks? Father was right. You *are* a poufter."

Undeterred by his sister's skepticism and homophobia, Vlad goes to work making Wallachia a kinder, gentler vassal state. In the castle courtyard, he replaces the gallows with an organic vegetable garden. He does away with his father's tradition of flogging three peasants every Friday morning. Instead, he prefers to tour the streets in a carriage, telling all of his subjects how much he and God love them. One subject says, "This young Vlad, he's certainly not the same kind of guy that his father was. Old Vlad would cut your throat if you looked at him the wrong way. This one just smiles and gives you a piece of quiche. It's not right. I expect my monarch to throw me down on the ground and beat me up. It's how things are done."

"Brother, you said that right," confirms his friend, the local dung salesman. "This new Vlad is really weird. All he does is stroke that cat of his. I wonder what the Turks are going to think of this caresser."

Unfortunately for the residents of Wallachia, twenty-thousand Turks under the leadership of Sub-Sultan Sydney the Sinful are on a tax-collecting ride in the Carpathians. Word had reached the sub-sultan of the old king's death, of the successful freelance raid, and of the young Vlad's ascension to the throne. As the Turks are finishing up a lovely morning spent burning a village to the ground and putting its residents to the sword, Sub-Sultan Sydney the Sinful says to his assistant sub-sultan, Ivan, "So, thank Allah old King Vlad the Destroyer is dead. That guy was a real pain in the ass. I heard that his kid's on throne. What's he like?"

"Well, Syd," replies the assistant sub-sultan, "he was raised in a monastery in England."

"Oh," says Sydney, "You mean he's a poufter."

"Yeah, probably. We shouldn't have trouble with Wallachia anymore. One of my spies tells me that all the new king wants to do is to have dinner parties and caress his cat."

"Caress his cat?"

"Yeah, the Wallachians are calling him 'Vlad the Caresser.'"

"In Allah's name. How 'bout that. Vlad the Destroyer is gone. And he's replaced with Vlad the Caresser. This is going to be fun." Sydney shouts orders to his army, and they begin the two-day ride to Vlad's castle.

When the young king hears from the sentinels about the approach of the Turkish army, he decides that he will not follow the lead of his father. Instead of ordering out the small Wallachian Defense Force, he'll have a dinner party for the Turks and invite them to listen to the Royal Light Opera Company, the *Transylvania 6-5000.*

Count Blasphemy, a former advisor to Vlad's father and Director of Homeland Security, comes into the Royal throne room and says, "Fuckin' ay, your majesty, I understand that you're in charge now, but I really don't get what you're doing.

We don't want to feed the Turks; we want to strangle them in their sleep."

"Count Blasphemy, watch your language, please. My cat, Innocent XVIII, is offended. Besides, we will do things differently during my reign. My father was a drunkard, fornicator, and murderer."

"Beggin' your fuckin' pardon, your highness, so he had a few faults."

"Count, my father was an abomination before God. And because of his evil, the Turks were visited upon us. I will make amends for my father's sins. The Turks will be so astonished by our goodness and quiche that they will immediately be converted to Christianity and join us as brothers in the Lord."

"Begging your fuckin' pardon again, your highness. I think you're out of your mind. The Turks aren't going to convert; they're going to slaughter us."

"Silence, Count Blasphemy," replies the gentle Vlad. "I tell you that we will overwhelm the Turks with our kindness."

"Couldn't we overwhelm them with boiling oil instead, your majesty?"

"Absolutely not. The crude methods of my father will not be tolerated."

"But they were very effective, your majesty."

"Only temporarily, Blasphemy. A kingdom based on fornication and hatred will always perish in the long run."

"Perhaps, your majesty, but it's a whole lot of fuckin' fun in the meantime."

"Oh, Blasphemy, will you never learn?" asks an exasperated Vlad. "The monks at Jarrow were also faced with barbarians at their gates. And how did they respond? Not with boiling oil, nor with vulgar words, nor with wanton sexuality. No, they responded with chaste love, with generosity, with Quiche Lorraine."

Count Blasphemy is doubtful, but he knows that the young Vlad signs his paycheck. "And these monks, your majesty, how did they fare? I suppose the Goths just turned tail and ran back to the continent, converted to the love of God and Jesus Christ."

"Well, actually they killed most of the monks and burned down six buildings. But that's not the point. The monks did the right thing. They just didn't trust enough in the Lord."

"They probably should have trusted in boiling oil."

"What was that, Count Blasphemy?"

"Nothing, your majesty. Nothing."

Two days later, the Turkish army arrives at the city. Syd and Ivan are a little shocked to find the castle gates wide open. On every building are hung giant banners saying, "Welcome Turks." Other banners proclaiming, "We salute Suleiman the Magnificent" hang from the castle walls. Syd is beside himself. "Don't these dolts know that we're the Turks? We're not the fucking Red Crescent. Don't they know that we don't take prisoners, that we're going to rape their women and plunder their gold?"

Ivan is a little shocked, too. He rubs his foot-long mustaches and says, "Weird, baby, weird." The streets of the city are lined with people holding flags with crescents. Staffed by masseuses recruited from throughout the kingdom, a new Turkish bath has been erected. Actually, the bath is a cesspool that the Chamber of Commerce cleaned up a little bit. But Vlad prides himself on his ability to improvise.

As the Turkish army makes its way up to the castle, it's met by a royal delegation led by Count Blasphemy. Behind the Count are several-dozen nuns. These women were formerly the old Vlad's concubines. But young Vlad told them that their only true lover would be Jesus Christ and that they should become his brides. At first the concubines were reluctant, and one of them asked Vlad whether Christ was a good kisser. The young king had been mortified, but trained by the ever-argumentative Brother Ignatius, Vlad had answered that the love that Christ gave was better than the best sex. A gasp went up from the concubines. And one of them asked, "Where do I sign up?" Within a couple of hours, the concubines were having their heads shaved and being put into habits and chastity belts.

The Count's party stops directly in front of the Turkish army. Trumpets sound, and Blasphemy, ad-libbing a little, reads from a royal proclamation. "Hear ye, fuckin' hear ye. Greetings in the fuckin' Lord. King Vlad the Caresser, son of Vlad the Destroyer, welcomes his Turkish brothers to Wallachia and invites them to partake of a Caesar salad and a Quiche Lorraine he has personally prepared."

Ivan leans over to Syd and says, "What the fuck is going on here? Why aren't they pouring boiling oil on our heads? I thought at least they would hurl boulders at us. What do you think?"

Syd replies in a low voice, "What do I think? I'll tell you what I think. I think that we're going to go eat some quiche and Caesar salad. Then we'll kill everyone."

A big smile spreads over Ivan's face.

In a loud voice, Syd replies to the invitation: "Tell your king that I, Sub-Sultan Sydney, third cousin twice removed from his eminence King Suleiman the Magnificent, would be very honored to eat his royal majesty."

Ivan leans over to Sydney and whispers in his ear: "With, you numbskull, eat with."

Sydney coughs loudly and says, "What I meant, of course, is that my chiefs and I would be very honored to dine with Vlad the Caresser and his royal entourage."

While Sydney is announcing his intention to break bread with Vlad, Sir Nasty, Count Blasphemy's aide-de-camp, shakes his head slowly. He leans over and speaks into the Count's ear: "I can't believe we're having dinner with these bastards. I don't even like Caesar salad. And what the hell is quiche? Shouldn't we be pouring boiling oil on these jerks? At least we ought to be thinking about ways to cut their throats in their sleep."

"Look," replies Count Blasphemy. "I don't fucking like this any better than you do. I'd love to kill them all, too. But you heard the chief: no boiling oil, no throat cutting."

"How about at least just one itsy-bitsy set of thumbscrews?"

"No, forget the thumbscrews. None of those either. Just quiche, Caesar salad, and some lemonade."

"Lemonade, why can't we have ale, like usual?"

"No ale. Vlad wants us to be able to have a good time without the influence of alcohol."

"But that's impossible."

"That's what I told him. He just said that we should be ourselves."

"But we're cold-blooded, thieving mercenaries."

"I told him that, too. He just said, 'Look inward and find the courage to be your true self, the self that the Lord always wanted you to be.'"

"Oh, god, he said that? The next thing he'll do is try to get us to give up sex."

"Well, you saw what he did with the concubines. This is definitely not his father's fucking kingdom."

The procession of infidel and Christian goes into the courtyard. When it arrives, the young king, standing in front of a giant crescent-shaped cake, greets his guests: "Welcome, my Turkish brothers. May I compliment you on the fineness of your mustaches. They are truly the best examples of tonsillary excellence that I have seen in some time."

"He's laying it on thick," Ivan whispers in Syd's ear. "Do you think that he really has archers lurking somewhere?"

"No, actually, I think he means it all. It's almost obscene. Isn't it?"

As the two sub-sultans dismount, Count Blasphemy eyes the huge scimitars hanging at the sides of the bodyguards. He whispers to Sir Nasty, "Let's keep our eyes open. I don't like the way things look right now. These guys seem hungry. If we're not careful, they may have us for dinner."

The two sultans get off their high horses and say hello to the king. And since they are asked to do so, they stroke

Innocent. But Syd hates anything feline, and Ivan is allergic to cats. Not particularly fond of infidels, Innocent hisses at both of the sultans. Sir Nasty thinks this a bad omen and starts to draw his sword, but Count Blasphemy steps on his foot.

The party of Christians and Turks sits down to dinner. Having never seen croutons before, Ivan picks one up and flings it at Sir Nasty, who again begins to draw his sword. "Later, later. Wait for it," Count Blasphemy whispers. After dinner, tea and scones are served, just as they had been at Jarrow. The catering staff presents finger bowls for everyone, and Sir Nasty begins drinking out of his, but Blasphemy steps on his foot again.

Nasty asks, "Why are you always picking on me, you shit?"

"Shut the fuck up," quietly replies the Count. "Have you no fucking sense of élan?"

Oblivious to this minor breach of etiquette, Vlad says, "My dear Turkish friends, I want this feast to be a symbol of a new relationship between my people and yours. For much too long, there has been enmity between our two nations."

"What does 'enmity' mean?" Sir Nasty quietly asks Count Blasphemy.

"It means we hate each other, you fucking idiot."

"Oh, that I understand," Sir Nasty replies. He smiles, revealing a bit of bacon lodged between two of his teeth.

Vlad III stops his speech, hangs his head, and says, "I must, on behalf of my father, apologize for the behavior of Wallachia toward the Turks. My father had many good qualities. Understanding and love of his fellow man were, unfortunately, not among them. I therefore apologize for the damage that my father has done. I know that he personally killed 7568 Turks."

"How does he know that?" asks Sir Nasty.

"Because old Vlad the fucking Destroyer kept a log."

"He certainly was thorough."

"Fucking ay."

Vlad continues: "I personally apologize for every single death that he caused. And I have decided that a mere apology is not enough. Since actions speak louder than words, I am starting the Wallachian Memorial College Fund. I firmly believe that education is the key to understanding. This fund will school free of charge any offspring or other surviving relatives of my father's victims. On behalf of the people of Wallachia and my dear departed father, I am personally donating to the fund twenty gold pieces for each of your people my father stabbed, strangled, decapitated, axed, drowned, eviscerated, burned, buried alive, or hanged."

"Remember the one he fucking tickled to death?" Blasphemy asks Nasty.

"Oh, yeah, I almost forgot. Why did he do that?"

"He wanted to prove that he had a sense of humor."

"He was such a card."

"My brothers," Vlad III says, "I implore you. Let the violence end. A new era of peaceful coexistence has begun. Let us unite in love, harmony, and pet ownership. What say you?"

Ivan's mouth is hanging open. He says to Syd, "I can't believe that this guy is for real. What do you think?"

Sultan Syd stands up and bows politely to the King, who smiles, strokes his cat, and returns the bow. "Your majesty," Syd replies. "I have only one thing to say." Vlad beams, expecting the sub-sultan to contribute twenty gold pieces to the college fund.

"Kill them all!" shouts Syd.

"Uh, oh!" Sir Nasty says, "Shit's going to hit the fan now."

"Yeah, it sure fuckin' is," replies Count Blasphemy, drawing his sword: "And remember to change the Anti-Turk Warning Alert from Amber to Red."

Soon the dining hall is a complete disaster. Fortunately for the Kingdom of Wallachia, Count Blasphemy had, unbeknownst to the King, stationed several of his best fighters under the serving tables. But the Turks outnumber the Wallachians about twelve to one. And to make matters even worse, Ivan finds Innocent XVIII in a chafing dish. Shouting "Die, Hell-spawn kitty," he impales the cat with a spare scimitar.

Count Blasphemy grabs the King and drags him away from the fighting. Vlad is crying hysterically: "My kingdom, my college fund, my kitty."

"It's fucking all right your majesty. We'll talk about things later." Then the Count locks the king into a secret vault deep within the castle. For the next several hours, bedlam reigns. Count Blasphemy, Sir Nasty, and their hand-picked soldiers manage to push the Turks out. But the cost to the kingdom is heavy. Almost all the Royal concubines have been carried off. Large parts of the town are in flames, and the money for the College Fund is speeding its way to Constantinople.

Riding off with a big smile on his face, Syd shouts: "'Brotherly love.' Hah, as soon as we get these concubines unlocked, we'll show you what love is all about. We'll be back."

Ivan adds: "And the quiche sucked."

Count Blasphemy goes down to the sub-basement and lets the king out of the vault. "How are you fucking doing, your majesty?"

The king is in tears: "My kitty, my kitty, they impaled my kitty. I offered my unconditional love, and this is what I get back. Why did this devastation happen?"

Count Blasphemy shakes his head: "Because you're a fucking goofball, your majesty. You can't love these people. They'll walk all over you. Now, your father may have been a royal bastard and cut off a few heads prematurely, but the Wallachians loved him, because when the Turks showed up at the fucking door, Old Vlad didn't give them chaste love and quiche. He got laid and hit them with everything he had. He wanted the Turks to be terrified of even thinking about coming to Wallachia. Okay, so he was a little out of control sometimes. There were the three vegetable salesmen he had drawn and quartered just because they were out of onions, but, hey, when the chips were down, you could always count on your dad."

"I can't believe that they impaled my kitty, poor Innocent. What did he do to them?" Vlad is crying tears of frustration. "What am I supposed to do? Maybe I should just go back to Jarrow. I can have chamomile tea every day, and I won't have to stand those smelly peasants anymore."

Count Blasphemy just stands there, shaking his head. "Oh, Christ," he thinks to himself. "This isn't going to work. I've got to snap the king out of this, or we're all going to end up as kebabs."

He picks Vlad up, dusts him off, and says, "Your majesty, I'm really sorry about what I'm going to do." He punches the king in the mouth, and Vlad crumples.

Count Blasphemy looks at the shocked young king and says, "Come on, your majesty, hit me back."

Vlad is blubbering. "I can't hit you. We must love our neighbors as ourselves."

"Oh, fucking hell," Count Blasphemy says, and he gives Vlad a swift kick. "What if your neighbors are fucking goobers, you majesty? Come on, hit me."

"I can't. I can't fight back. It's not right. Please stop. I'll make you a nice quiche if you do."

"Okay," says Count Blasphemy, "have it your way." He gives the king another kick. "You know, I don't even like quiche. In fact, I fucking hate it." He reaches down, slapping the king.

At this moment, the course of Wallachian history changes forever. Vlad climbs to his feet and says, "You bastard." Then he hits Blasphemy as hard as he can.

The Count is turned around by the blow, which lands squarely on his nose. He shakes himself off, faces the king, and smiles, the blood gushing out of both nostrils. "Way to fucking go, your majesty. That was great. I'll make a murdering tyrant out of you yet."

"But I hit you. It was wrong. Brother Ignatius told me that it's always wrong to hit someone."

Count Blasphemy answers: "Well, Brother Ignatius is fucking safe in a monastery. He doesn't have twenty-thousand screaming Turks who want to turn him into a shish kebab. Praying is fine for monks. But you're not a monk. You're the son of Vlad the fucking Destroyer. Now be a man and take responsibility for yourself."

Vlad feels different, somehow freer. He stops crying and says to Blasphemy: "Maybe you're right. Maybe it should be a fucking eye for a fucking eye."

Blasphemy smiles. "Thank god," he thinks, "maybe we're getting somewhere." He says to the King, "Very good, your fucking majesty. Come with me. There's something else you need to do."

"What's that?" asks Vlad.

"To come."

"I don't understand."

"Don't worry. You will. It's what your father would have wanted."

With Count Blasphemy holding a torch to cut through the gloom, the two men walk out of the room and down an inky-black passage. They arrive at another vault, and Count Blasphemy opens the door. Inside sits Hildegard, the youngest and cutest of the old king's concubines.

"How are you doing, Hildy?"

"I'm scared."

"Don't worry, the Turks have fucking left, and the king is going to lead a bloodthirsty raid against them in a little while."

"He is?" asks Hildegard, aware of the king's proclivity for quiche and stand against violence.

"He is."

"I am?" asks Vlad.

"You are. You'll be fine. But first I want you to get to

know your father's favorite concubine. Hildy, your young king here's in need of a little instruction in the ways of the fucking world, if you know what I mean."

"But I already know four languages," says Vlad. "I can recite all of the offices of the breviary. And I know astronomy and algebra."

"Yeah, but can you give a good hickey?" Hildegard asks.

"What's a hickey?"

"That's what you're about to find out, you fucking lucky dog, I mean your majesty," Blasphemy says. "Hildy, be good to him. Your majesty, consider Hildegard here to be a teacher."

"Oh, Blasphemy, aren't you forgetting something?" asks Hildegard.

"Right, my mistake," he answers. He tosses Hildegard the key to her chastity belt. "Have fun, you two. I'll be back in a couple of fucking hours to collect the king."

Count Blasphemy gently shuts the door and walks up out of the castle's sub-basement. The scene is a mess. The Turks have decapitated three priests and thrown their heads on top of the giant cake. Not only did the visitors from the East burn most of the wooden buildings, they also spray-painted a message for the young King on the side of the castle. "Vlad Sucks." Little do the Turks know.

Sir Nasty is in the process of torturing two prisoners in order to find out which road the Turkish column has taken. Seeing the Count walking toward him, he shouts, "Hey there, Blasphemy. Where have you been?"

"Well, while you've been having fucking fun there"—he motions to the two screaming Turks—"I've been trying to get us a real king. After kicking him around for a little bit, I actually got him to get angry enough to hit me back. Now I've got him in a vault with Hildegard. She'll make a man out of him."

"No shit. Well, things might actually turn out all right. I discovered from our two friends that their army will be going through the Valley of Despair. If we can get a few hundred men together, we might be able to head them off at the pass and plan a little trap for them."

"Good work, Nasty. I knew that if anyone could get information out of these assholes, it would be you. Why don't you start rounding men up? Anybody who can carry a sword would be great."

A few hours later, about four hundred men sit on horses, waiting to ride out and ambush the Turks. "We're ready to go. Where's the king?" asks Nasty.

"I'll go check on him. Do you have it?"

"Yup, right here." Nasty holds up the scimitar on which is impaled Vlad's ex-cat, Innocent XVIII.

"Fucking wonderful," Count Blasphemy says. "That should really piss him off. I'll go see if we have us a fucking king."

Count Blasphemy walks back through the rubble in the courtyard. He then goes downstairs and opens the vault. Vlad and Hildegard are under a blanket together. Vlad has a great big smile on his face, and Hildegard sports on her neck a giant hickey.

"How did it go, you two?"

Hildegard smiles and says, "He's his father's son and a great kisser. He even bit me on the neck."

Blasphemy beams. "Your father would be proud of you, Vlad. How do you feel, your majesty?"

"Great, Brother Ignatius never said that sins of the flesh could be so good."

"Yeah, your majesty, they're some of the best sins we've got going here on earth. Well, now that you've gotten laid, are you ready to go kill some Turks?"

"I don't know, Blasphemy. Maybe we should just stay here. We can strengthen the town's defenses for their next attack."

"No, no, your majesty. That's not it at all. We have to hit the Turks with everything we have. If they think that we won't retaliate, they'll come back again and again. Unless we strike now, they'll think that they can get away with this." Count Blasphemy suddenly produces from behind his back the scimitar on which poor Innocent XVIII hangs.

Hildegard passes out at the sight. And Vlad himself grows pale. At first he becomes very quiet. Then, with a barely controlled hatred, he says, "Let's get them. I want to do the same thing to them that they did to my innocent kitty."

"Now, you're fucking talking, your majesty." Blasphemy reaches around to the outside of doorway. "Here's your weapon." He hands Vlad a huge, flat broad sword.

Vlad says, "My father was right, and Brother Ignatius was wrong. You just can't show these people any mercy. I don't think that they even liked my quiche."

Count Blasphemy replies, "No, your majesty. I distinctly heard one of the sultans say, 'This really sucks.'"

"Well, that's it, then. They hate my cooking, kill my people, and impale my kitty. By the memory of my rather truculent father, I swear that by the end of the day, Sub-Sultan Sydney will be impaled on this sword."

"Now you're fucking talking, your majesty. Your dear old dad would have been fucking proud of you."

The two men leave the still prostrate Hildy in the vault and walk into the courtyard, where the small army waits. Vlad steps up on a pile of wood and addresses the group: "Men, I want you to know that we are about to open a new period of Wallachian history. No longer will I be styled 'Vlad the Caresser,' gentle but ineffective leader of the Wallachians. The peacemakers may be blessed, but they almost always have their quiche thrown back in their faces. No longer will the Turks be met with kindness and understanding. From now on, they will meet only the sword." The men cheer wildly. Vlad goes on: "From this day forward, I will be known as 'Vlad the Impaler,' implacable foe of the Turk. Our enemy can expect no mercy from us, especially as he is guilty of such treachery." The men gasp as Vlad holds up the kitty-kebab. "No longer will we tolerate such feline defilement."

Sir Nasty, who has been listening quietly, says to the Count: "Well, he has a great vocabulary, even if he is a poufter."

"He isn't a poufter anymore. He just got fucking laid."

"No, really?"

"Fucking ay. He and Hildegard got together for a couple of hours."

"Hildy? I've been trying to get under her peasant skirt for months."

"What can I fuckin' say? It's good to be the king."

While Count Blasphemy and Sir Nasty discuss the king's recent loss of his virginity, the army becomes ecstatic when it realizes that the fate of Wallachia now rests in the hands of a violent control freak. The men rally around their king, chanting, "Vlad, Vlad, Vlad."

The young king holds up his hands. "Silence, my brave warriors. The time for talking is through. What we need now is mayhem. Are you with me?"

In unison, the soldiers shout, "Yes."

Vlad replies, "To the open road."

"Fucking ay," yells Count Blasphemy.

The small army rides out from the castle. Within a few hours, it finds the Turks at a rest stop along the Trans-Transylvanian Highway. A pitched battle ensues. Even though the Wallachians are hopelessly outnumbered, they fight like men possessed. Vlad himself kills a hundred-and thirty-five Turks. He even personally skewers Syd the Sub-Sultan, whose dying words are, "I still think your cooking sucks." The remaining Turks ride off towards the border.

Vlad decapitates all the dead Turks and puts their heads on spears lining the highway. "This will scare the shit out of them for years to come," Vlad proclaims to his cheering men.

"Fucking ay," affirms Count Blasphemy, always ready to add a helpful few words to the king's messages.

Thus was born the legend of Vlad Dracul, the killer of Turks, the impaler of heads, and the maker of a really good quiche. Unfortunately, Bram Stoker—never fond of French cooking— left out the quiche part when he wrote his novel.

But more important than quiche is what self-denial did for the people of Wallachia: not very much. It was only when their young king embraced his desires that life took a turn for the better. Of course, the young Vlad ended up killing 123,493 of his own citizens in the process of protecting them. But, hey, what's a little collateral damage when you're keeping homeland security high?

What not to do

There are steps that you can take to make sure that you never find yourself in the position in which the young Vlad Dracul was.

1. Don't put off until tomorrow what you can do today.

Generally, this slogan suggests industriousness. But its real meaning is that you should do exactly what you want, right now, without thinking about the consequences of your action. (For examples of famous people who gave themselves permission to enjoy, see *Table Eight.*) So, if you want to have that extra ham-and-cheese sandwich, go ahead and have it. You'll feel better. After all, you can count calories when you're dead.

2. Don't save any money.

Saving money is a way to get yourself out of the situation you're in. The trouble is that if everyone saved money instead of going deeply into debt, the economy—based as it is on consumption—would collapse in about twenty minutes. So, what seems like a good thing is actually the worst possible action to take. Spend your money—and everybody else's—as freely as possible.

3. Don't think about tomorrow.

Rather, concern yourself only with the present. When you start thinking about the future, you actually screw things up pretty badly. You'll start making action plans, and we've already seen how damaging they can be. Tomorrow will arrive without your help. So, don't spend your time trying to rack up spiritual bonus points for some distant future that might not actually materialize. Enjoy yourself in the here and now. §

Table Eight: Famous Individuals Who Learned to Give themselves Permission to Enjoy

Famous Individual	Item(s) Enjoyed
Eve	Apples
Judas Iscariot	Silver
Mohammed	"The entire earth at my feet, you infidels!"
Genghis Kahn	"The entire earth, including you presumptuous Muslims, at my feet!"
Kaiser Wilhelm II	Pointy hats
Sigmund Freud	Long cigars
Robert Oppenheimer	Chain reactions
Donald Trump	Cheap Atlantic-City real estate
Henry Kissinger	Carpet bombing
William Jefferson Clinton	Monica, French Fries, French women, Queen Elizabeth, Elizabeth Shue, Shoe-Fly Pie, Anne, Kelly, Kelly-Anne, Anne-Kelly, Grace Kelly, Grace Jones, Paula Jones, Joanie and Chachi (with Chachi just watching)

Chapter 8:

The Myth of Diversity

One of the most prevalent myths of our time is that of diversity, which holds that we should celebrate the differences in others, that those who are different bring us new values and original ways to look at the world. While there's absolutely nothing untrue about this philosophy, it begs an important question: do we really want new ways to look at the world? Despite all of our assertions, I'm not sure that we do. Why? Because people who really are different from us pose a threat. If we looked at the world through somebody else's eyes, we just might find that our own vision is skewed. And we might feel compelled to take steps to correct the mess that we see. Most people who talk about diversity generally mean either market segmentation or a gathering of well-educated, docile, and career-oriented people of all flavors and shades. Real diversity, with people who are nothing like us, is a completely different animal.

College campuses aside, the location in which diversity makes the biggest impact is the workplace. In order to see what true diversity might mean at the office, let's examine "Worktopia," the diversity initiative of the J.B. Downing Medical Publishing House, a subsidiary of Marcourt, Race, and Boganovich. The proponent of this initiative is none other than J.B. Downing himself. J.B. is a domineering man who likes to stroll the cubicle-lined corridors of his place of business while listening to *The Ode to Joy* on a Walkman.

One day J.B. watches two of his workers—one white and one black—talking by the water cooler. J.B. decides that mere diversity of race, age, and gender is not enough. Later, he and Bob DeLucca, J.B.'s Human Resources Manager, are sitting together at either end of the giant conference table in J.B.'s private room. "By god," he tells Bob, "bring me people who are really different. It's a big world that we live in. Bring me the huddled masses. Bring me the lunatic fringe." On the walls of the conference room hang portraits of Attila the Hun, Joseph Stalin, and Richard Branson. He continues: "By god, Bob, if we pull this off, they'll bring me to Boston and make me a partner in the firm—a partner. Do you have any idea of the stock options involved here? Not only that, but with the power of a partnership behind me, I'll be able to enact my strategic vision of having all Marcourt books include a medical addendum. Imagine, *The Collected Works of George Orwell* with an excursus on colon cancer. The mind reels, Bob, the mind reels." J.B. touches a button under the conference table, and *The Ode to Joy* begins to play over the loudspeakers.

Bob agrees that the mind does indeed reel. At least J.B.'s mind does. But Bob has a boy whose overbite needs correcting and a girl who wants to study the works of Emily Bronte at a really expensive East Coast college. And so, over the din of *The Ode to Joy*, Bob asks, "What exactly do you have in mind, J.B.?"

J.B. takes a cigar from the stash in a drawer in the conference-room table. The room in which the table sits had once been used by the previous occupants of the building—*The Saturday Evening Post*—to hold discussions with Norman Rockwell about how cherry the cheeks of the subjects in his paintings were to be. J.B. cuts the end of the cigar. "Robert, my boy," he says to Bob—who is fifty-seven-years old, two years older than J.B.—"I want our diversity initiative to be as big as this cigar. Actually, I would like our initiative to include Cuban tobacco growers. I suppose that we can't always get exactly what we want. Well, generally, I get exactly what I want. But, hell, sometimes I suppose we can make exceptions." He lights the cigar and exhales a long, thin plume of smoke as he looks out a window onto Independence Square in Philadelphia.

"Just think, Robert, my boy, many big ideas, some of the biggest, originated right here, just across the street. This is a place of intellectual fermentation. You can smell it."

Actually, Bob can't smell very much besides the smoke from J.B.'s cigar. Downing continues: "The Declaration of Independence, the Constitution: they both began right here, and look at how they changed the world."

Bob's prostate is sensitive to demagoguery. At that moment it announces its presence. He sighs and responds, "J.B., it certainly sounds as if your diversity initiative will have a profound impact on our way of doing business. Why don't you give me the details?"

"I like your attitude, Robert. I like it very much." Actually, J.B. doesn't like anything about Bob, save his dog-like willingness to carry out—in return for a ridiculously low salary—any ludicrous plan that he—J.B.— might develop.

"'Worktopia' is the name of it." (For a list of famous diversity initiatives throughout history, see *Table Nine*.)

Table Nine: Historical Examples of Diversity in the Workplace

Project/ organization	Visionary Leader	Elements of Diverse Population Employed
Construction of Pyramids	Amenhotep	Egyptian slaves, Jewish slaves, Chaldean slaves, Coptic slaves, Lebanese slaves
Spanish Inquisition	Torquemada	Angry priests, frustrated priests, enraged priests, sadistic priests, disillusioned priests
Staffing of Eighteenth-Century British Navy	Lord Nelson	Sailors kidnapped from United States, sailors kidnapped from England, sailors kidnapped from Canada, sailors kidnapped from Mexico, sailors kidnapped from France
Construction of American Trans-Continental Railroad	Leland Stanford and others	Destitute Chinese, destitute Irish, destitute Indians, destitute Italians, destitute Poles
New Economic Plan	V.I. Lenin	Political dissidents, religious dissidents, literary dissidents, intellectual dissidents, not-so-intellectual dissidents
Construction of Fortress Europe	Albert Speer	Jewish slaves, gypsy slaves, homosexual slaves, Allied slaves, socialist slaves
D-Day Landings at Omaha Beach	Dwight D. Eisenhower	Terrified soldiers, conscripted soldiers, drunk soldiers, patriotic soldiers (see drunk soldiers), soldiers who thought that the boats were going to Coney Island for the weekend

"Worktopia," repeats the fawning Bob Dog. "It's fantastic, J.B., just out of this world." Bob really thinks that it sounds like the title of a science fiction novel, one featuring aliens who kidnap fifty-seven-year-old men, snip their prostates, and then whisk the prisoners off to Planet Worktopia. There they spend the rest of their lives growing bulgur wheat. Either that or the name is akin to something that he vaguely remembers from his college days, when he was reading from a labor history book in fulfillment of one of the requirements for his B.S. in organizational behavior. "Worktopia" strikes him as something from a labor movement or something that the Public Interest Research Groups or Greenpeace would develop.

Moreover, it sounds dangerous to him, since it hints at workers' rights. And one thing that was drummed into his head in the "Human Resources Management" course that he had taken was that workers possess absolutely no rights. Nor, emphasized his professor, "should they ever be told that they might have rights. Rather, they should be instructed that their very lives—sorry as they are—possess only one purpose, and that is to generate profits for the company. They are destined to be cogs in the wheel, nothing more and nothing less. Cogs in a giant wheel that rolls perpetually in service to the Fuehrer...er, excuse me, in service to the corporation, my mistake." This professor of German extraction had joined the new organizational-theory department under mysterious circumstances in late April of 1945.

Against his own better judgment, Bob says, "Worktopia, that sounds like a fantastic idea. Tell me more, J.B. I want to make sure that my actions are in accord with your sharp vision."

"Robert, my boy," J.B. says in response to Bob's stroking, "you'll go far in this company. You'll be my right-hand man." Bob notes to himself that J.B. is left-handed. "You'll implement the plan and see it through to completion. Some of us," he says. He pauses and gestures to the picture of Francisco Franco that he had installed on the wall on the day of the Generalissimo's demise in 1976. "There are some of us who are destined to leave our marks on society through our vision. And there are others," he says, pointing the cigar at Bob, "who will not leave their individual marks, but who serve others' destinies. I am of the former type. And you are of the latter. Don't you find it wonderful that fate, no, not fate, call it Zeitgeist, has thrown us together?" Bob's prostate really begins to act up. But he nods dutifully.

J.B. stretches in his chair and then continues: "Let me tell you about Worktopia. Whereas other companies pay lip service to diversity by hiring a few niggers, spics, and fags, we'll go them one better. Besides, we already have our quota of niggers, spics, and fags, don't we?"

"Yes, J.B., you're right. But you probably should be careful when you use those derogatory names."

"Listen, you little Guinea, don't you ever correct my language again. If you do, I'll send you back to Wopland where you came from. Just stroke my ego. That's your job. Do you understand me?"

"Yes, J.B. Our statistics are fantastic, and the staff has begun to reflect the ethnicity and gender of the servants that our physician/customers employ. Despite the meager salaries that we offer, we've attracted a compliant and docile workforce, a real melting pot. Through lying about advancement opportunities and secretly refusing to give good references to anyone who wants to leave the company, we've established a terrific employee-retention rate."

"Excellent, excellent, Robert, my boy. I like your can-do attitude. And I especially like your use of the term 'melting pot.' That image will form the core of our approach. By the way, do you know how the term originated?"

Bob flounders for a moment and then says, "Well, J.B., I always assumed it had something to do with stew, with soup. You take many different ingredients, cup them up, and put them in the melting pot. Each ingredient adds its own unique taste to the overall flavor of the soup." Bob formed this opinion by watching several episodes of *School House Rock* in the mid-1970s.

J.B. looks at Bob with eyes that are simultaneously piercing and devoid of any sign of intelligence. And he says, slowly, "Soup, soup." Then he explodes, "Wrong, Alpobreath! Melting pot comes from the steel factories of the nineteenth-century visionaries. Raw iron would be brought in and dropped into huge pots in which it would be melted. This country was made great through the destruction of individuality and its transformation into something of value, into wealth."

As he says this last word, J.B. takes a deep drag on the cigar and lets out another breath. "Wealth" is a word that really appeals to him, one of those words that its user has made into a fetish, tuned into something more than a word, transformed into a vessel that carries more than most words ever can.

"Wealth," he says again.

"Wealth," duly echoes Bob.

The word "wealth" boings around the room and finally boings out the window into the stratosphere, where, carrying a tinge of cigar smoke, it travels into the far reaches of the solar system.

"Anyway," says J.B., "a melting pot is very much what I have in mind. The raw ingredients, the ingots of industry, will be transformed into the product of profit."

Bob goes over to the flip chart in the corner of the room. He writes "ingots of industry" in big letters. He draws a set of downward-pointing double arrows. Then he writes the second phrase: "product of profit."

"What I want you to do," says J.B., "is to hire as many different kinds of people as possible."

"What do you mean by 'different'?" asks Bob.

"What I mean, you numbskull, is for you to sweep the Bowery."

Bob isn't even sure if the Bowery exists anymore.

"Go to the prisons. Visit the union halls."

Bob, because of the conditioning he has been subjected to in his Human Resources training, breaks into a cold sweat each time he hears the word "union."

"Bring me the most unique people in the world. Bring me graduate students in Chaucer, and bring me black Muslims from North Philadelphia. Bring me Wobblies. Bring me Wookies. Bring me all of this and more."

J.B. puts down his cigar and picks up a shepherd's crook that he keeps in a corner of the room. He bought it while making a retreat at the St. Raoul monastery and gift shop in France. Again he touches the button under the conference table. This time the sound track from *The Ten Commandments* erupts from the speakers.

"That's right, Robert, me lad. J.B. will lead his chosen people to the salvation of Worktopia, where we will all labor in service to the God of Profit, and there will be a second coming of the Dow Jones Industrials. The stock market will hit 100,000. And J.B. will be made a partner in the firm of Marcourt, Race, and Boganovich. In the back of *The Collected Works of George Orwell* will be that excursus on colon cancer. I can just see it right now," J.B. says. "Can't you?"

Bob can in fact picture it, and the thought of J.B. exercising pastoral leadership over the dregs of society, over the collective corporate flotsam and jetsam, scares him to death. Bob can already see J.B. leading of a body of really strange people—like the guys with flashing palms in *Logan's Run*. Bob's skin begins to crawl.

J.B. steps away from the conference table and kneels. "Bob," he says, "before you go back out into the workplace to implement my plan, I want you to pray with me for the success of Worktopia." Bob isn't very religious. But he realizes that when J.B. is in one of his moods, it is in his—Bob's—best interest to go along with the scheme. The two men kneel in front of the portrait of Attila the Hun as J.B. leads the prayer: "Dear Heavenly Father, please let our Worktopia initiative succeed. Let us be successful in our endeavor to attain a partnership and to spread the word that all human resources can be melted down into the product of pure profit. We ask this, in your name. Amen."

J.B. then looks at Bob and says, "The meeting is ended. Go in peace to love and serve your boss." The CEO of Downing

Medical Publishing House then returns to the table and presses the secret button. The strains of *The Ode to Joy* once again fill the conference room. J.B. closes his eyes and waves Bob away.

Silently, Bob leaves the conference room and walks down the hall into the netherworld of the cubicle-strewn production floor, which is bathed in a strange, incandescent light.

Bob says, "Thank god I don't have to sit in one of those fucking things." He goes to his office with a window that also overlooks Independence Square, and he asks his half-black, half-Hispanic, half-Jewish, half-Inuit, and half-Sikh assistant, Alberta Murcheson, to join him. She walks in and plops down into the chair in front of Bob's desk. He looks at her and realizes, as he occasionally does, that she—with her M.A. in Swahili from Brown, is much more highly educated than he. He wonders whether she secretly has designs on his job, just as he has designs on J.B.'s position. And he makes a mental note to himself that her evaluation this year, which would be glowing, should not be too glowing. He would give her "Needs Improvement" in one or two categories, nothing too terrible, but just enough to make sure that she would be kept in her place, and, consequently, that he would be kept in his. He would say that her filing—which is impeccable—doesn't cut the mustard. Specifically, he would say that she often places 'M' files under 'Mc', something which in actuality she has never once done.

"Alberta," he says, "J.B. and I have come up with a new initiative, something that will bring us greater glory and make J.B. Downing the leader in diversity."

"Wonderful," Alberta says, none too enthusiastically. Bob makes another mental note to write "Moody" in the personality section of Alberta's file.

That will fix her multiethnic wagon, Bob thinks. "Alberta, we are going to have a workplace like none other in the industry."

"We already do."

"How do you mean?"

"We already lead most industries in terms of lowness of salaries and terribleness of benefits."

"Yes, Alberta, it's true. J.B. and I certainly have accomplished a great deal. But we want to take our success to the next level."

"You're not going to offer any benefits at all and make the employees rent their own cubicle space?"

"Alberta is nobody's fool," Bob thinks. "I'll have to watch her. With ideas like those, she could be a corporate vice president in six months. I'll really have to do a number on her personnel record."

"No, Alberta, although those are not bad suggestions. Why don't you draft a memo from me to J.B. and include them in it? But the real reason I've called you in is to have you start a recruiting campaign unlike any other. I want to change the advertisements that we usually run. When you compose the ad for copy editor, for example, you should say, "Members of Communist Party of America especially encouraged to apply." For the Help-Desk position, list the usual qualifications and then add: "We encourage Fundamentalist Muslims, especially those involved in Fatwahs, in the workplace." And for the production manager position, let's hire a Wobblie."

Alberta is quick to see which way the wind is breaking. She adds, "And for the technology-group positions, we can say, 'Mujahadeen especially encouraged to apply.'"

Bob is terrified of being outdone by his all-too-bright assistant. And he responds with just a hint of caution in his voice: "Excellent idea, Alberta, excellent idea."

"And I have another one. Let's have a member of the IRA as our new acquisitions editor. We definitely want to get the separatist position on otolaryngology."

"Yes, yes, Alberta. But don't forget to make sure that his or her new assistant is a member of the Royal Ulster Constabulary. Remember the words of J.B.: "The lion shall sleep with the lamb." All people will find a corporate home at

J.B. Downing. The raw material of human resources will be melted down and form the steel-hard commodity of increased Net Asset Values."

Alberta thinks that the whole initiative is just another stupid plot spawned by rapacious white men who have nothing better to do with their time. But she chimes in, "Amen, Brother Bob. And I think that I'll make sure that our new Internet editor position is staffed by a Luddite."

Not wanting to turn down a chance to fake inclusiveness, Bob replies, "Amen, Alberta, I be down with that."

Alberta is a Roman Catholic who speaks perfect French and has a B.A. from Georgetown. She's appalled by Bob, but she knows enough to go along with Whitey when he's busy being condescending: "I know you be, Brother Bob. I know you be."

Six months later, J.B. Downing is at the Philadelphia International Airport, returning from his annual six-week vacation to the Caribbean. Also at the airport is Franklin Boganovich, chief executive officer of Marcourt, Race, and Boganovich. Franklin is the son of the company's founder, Walter Boganovich, who taught Franklin the most important lesson to be learned in publishing — Never enter into contract negotiations with a sober author. "Liquor him up good, boy, liquor him up good," Franklin would say at the end of the story that cheerfully recounted the occasion when his father was able to purchase from William Faulkner the rights to *The Sound and the Fury* for a fourteen-dollar advance against three percent royalties.

"I just poured another double bourbon into him and said, 'Bill, that's all there is to it. Ain't worth a penny more. Have yourself another slug and sign the paperwork.' The poor bastard was so snookered that he said, 'Oh, the hell with it. You're probably right, Walt, sounds fair to me.' Then he passed out. We made a cool six million on that deal and had a forty-two percent margin."

Having inherited the calculating nature of his father,

Franklin Boganovich boldly took the company into the world of ladies' undergarments, which, while not as prestige-laden as *The Collected Works of George Orwell*, certainly produced a nice net margin.

Franklin had been skeptical when J.B. had sent him the e-mail announcing the premiere of Worktopia, but he realized that J.B. had consistently produced a twenty-seven percent gross margin by underpaying his overqualified workers and by using the shoddiest materials he could find, all the while espousing empty phrases such as "total quality management" and "customer satisfaction." J.B. was a rare gem. And so, Franklin had given Corporate approval for the initiative. "If anybody knows how to get money out of a project," he told his partners Race and Marcourt, "it's J.B. Let's really give him some leeway here. If hiring a few anarchists will make the company look like it cares about anything except its bottom line and bring us an increased margin, hell, Worktopia's for me. If it works at Downing, then maybe all of the MRB companies will implement it."

Having not heard anything from Downing in a while, Franklin decided to go to Philadelphia and see for himself how the initiative was progressing, how the raw material of humanity was being melted down in the cauldron of the workplace into steel-hard profits.

As the two men meet in Baggage Claim, Franklin notices with envy Downing's deep and even tan. He makes a mental note to himself to knock down J.B.'s usually glowing review by just one notch. How dare J.B., just a vice president at a mere subsidiary, have a deeper tan than he, a partner in the holding company. But, Franklin supposes, if J.B.'s initiative is really working, then almost anything can be forgiven.

"J.B.," Franklin greets his underling, "You're looking wonderful."

J.B. genuflects once and then vigorously pumps the hand of Boganovich. "It's great to see you, Franklin. I'm so glad that you could take some time from your incredibly busy schedule in Massachusetts to come down and see how Worktopia is progressing here in the City of Brotherly Love."

"J.B., I always enjoy getting out of Boston and visiting our medical business. And I expect nothing less than perfection from your Worktopia. If anybody can produce perfection, I know that it's you, J.B."

As the limousine races from the airport, J.B. and Franklin talk about how Worktopia is going. "It's been pretty quiet here," Franklin says, admiring the new pinky ring his wife had just bought him. "I haven't heard very much from Philadelphia lately."

"Well," says J.B., "I sent Bob an e-mail on Friday before I left the island. I'm sure that he's busy finishing up everything here. He's been my right-hand man throughout this whole process. And I'm positive that Worktopia will be in full swing by the time that we arrive."

The car roars through the No-man's Land of oil refineries between the airport and Center City Philadelphia. Franklin says, "Ah, look at all this, power, sheer power. It's beautiful, isn't it?"

J.B. agrees that it is in fact gorgeous. The car roars onto I-676 for the final leg of the journey into Center City. Then it pulls up to the front of the Curtin Building. Franklin and J.B. get out of the car and walk up the white imitation-marble steps.

"Franklin," J.B. says as he opens the door for his boss and soon-to-be partner: "Welcome to Worktopia."

Franklin's eyes go wide at what he sees. Inside the front door is a small bunker made out of sandbags. Smoke drifts through the air, making it difficult to breathe. Alberta Murcheson is wearing a combat helmet. She sticks her head out of the bunker opening. "Mr. Downing, Mr. Boganovich, how lovely to see you. Bob told me that you'd be returning, Mr. Downing, and that you'd be visiting, Mr. Boganovich. It's a pleasure to meet you, sir."

J.B. looks at the smoke through which the powerful

emergency lights cut. Alberta darts back into the bunker for a moment and emerges with two flak jackets. She hands them to J.B. and Franklin.

J.B. asks, "Alberta, what's going on here? And where's Bob?"

"Well, sir, we've been having a little trouble with Worktopia since you left. Bob is in the mail room negotiating."

"Negotiating," Franklin says, looking puzzled, "this is an at-will employer. We don't negotiate with workers."

"In this case, we had to, sir."

"Who is he negotiating with?" J.B. asks.

"The Zapatistas."

Franklin looks at J.B. and says, "The Zapatistas. They're terrorists."

"Freedom fighters, sir," says Alberta, "depending on your point of view."

"And they're fine workers, Franklin," J.B. adds.

From the extreme end of the building comes a whistling sound.

Alberta shouts, "Incoming!" and then calmly says, "Gentlemen, I suggest that you step into the bunker for a moment. It seems that Bob was unable to broker an end to the 9:00 a.m. mortar attacks."

An explosion rocks the lobby. The emergency lights blink off for a moment then wink back on.

"Mortar attack," Franklin says. "Will someone please tell me what the hell is going on here? I expected to find a twenty-eight percent gross margin, not a reenactment of *A Bridge Too Far*."

"I assure you, sir, that it's not a reenactment," Alberta says. "We took a casualty yesterday. A bike courier who was unaware of the timing of the mortar attacks was eviscerated."

"Good god," J.B. says. "They seemed so happy right before I left. What happened?"

"Well, sir, it seems that one of the former PRI agents that Bob hired told one of the Zapatistas that Marcos is, and I quote, sir, 'a sack of shit.' The mortar attacks started immediately afterwards."

Visibly shaken, J.B. looks at Franklin, who swings his head back and forth slowly. Franklin mumbles, "No margin, no margin. Where did my margin go?"

In the background, music plays softly. And a strangely acrid smoke begins to drift into the hallway. Franklin sniffs twice and throws up in the corner of the bunker. J.B., who is on the verge of retching, asks, "What the hell is that?" Just as he finishes his question, a wail, half in pain, half in mourning, sounds.

"Suttee, sir," says Alberta, who's fitted herself with a pair of nose clips.

"What's Suttee?" asks J.B., between fits of coughing.

"It's a form of human sacrifice, sir, used principally in India before the installation of the British Raj. Whenever a rich man would die, the wife would be burned along with him on the funeral pyre."

"You mean they're burning someone?" J.B. asks.

"Yes, sir," answers Alberta, "but don't worry, she's just a production assistant. I started advertising her position in the papers yesterday."

In between spells of retching and with a handkerchief across his mouth, Franklin says, "Good god, J.B., this Worktopia is an unmitigated disaster."

J.B. is crestfallen. He sees his partnership go up in smoke along with the production assistant. Out of the gloom emerges Bob. He wears a helmet and leaps from cubicle to cubicle.

"Hello, J.B.," says Bob as he springs into the bunker. "How are you? Hello, Franklin." Still retching, Boganovich merely waves.

"Gentlemen," Bob warns, "be careful of the land mines. We think the antipersonnel mines were the work of the Zapatistas."

J.B. is aghast. "Suttee and human immolation, how could all of this have happened? Why don't we send out a company-wide e-mail calling for calm?"

Alberta says, "We can't, sir. The internal server is down. We think that one of the Mossad agents destroyed it after the Neo-Nazis in Systems Support started sending hate e-mail. When you opened the document, a giant Swastika appeared, and then a kazoo version of *Deutschland Uber Ales* began playing on the computer speakers."

"Oh, my god," wails Downing, "This is terrible. Why isn't the brilliant human raw material being melted down in the cauldron of the workplace into the steel-hard profits as I had envisioned?"

"Because you're an ass, J.B.," says Franklin. "Don't you realize that profits aren't based on brilliance and divergent opinions, but on mindless obedience to authority? We don't want our employees to think or express themselves, except in very limited, narrowly defined ways, ways that will cause us no harm. I should have seen this coming. J.B., you're fired. Bob, you've mindlessly obeyed orders, and so have you, Alberta. You've both flawlessly executed a plan without regard for its disastrous potential outcome. There are places for both of you in this organization."

Franklin immediately takes command of the situation. He fires the Zapatistas, the Neonazis, the Orthodox rabbis, and all the rest of the recalcitrant human resources. In their place he hires twenty-two-year old art history majors with massive student loans. Profits once again soar.

Bob's prostate problem quiets down with the scrapping of Worktopia, and he's given J.B.'s job. Alberta's composure, elan, and the jaunty tilt of her helmet earn her a full partnership at Marcourt.

Thus is diversity. It does not mean different flavors of human ice cream. It means tangible differences. It means people with vastly different points of view who might not like each other.

What not to do

Do you want to live surrounded by people who really don't like you and whom you can't stand? Of course you don't. There are simple and concrete steps you can not take to ensure that your life will be free of people whose very existence grates on your nerves.

1. Don't ever travel overseas, unless you're on a package tour.

The directors of package cruises, flights, and bus trips go to great lengths to make certain that their patrons don't come into contact with foreign nationals who might have the temerity to be poor and hungry. "Too many distended stomachs spoil the buffet," is an accepted maxim in the world of recreation directors. These directors also go out of their way to protect their charges from the unpleasantries associated with chance encounters with people whose close relatives have died at the hands of joyriding marines in Italy. In Cancun, Mexico, cruise directors also try to keep their guests away from the quite diverse and unaccountably upset Chiapan rebels. These ingrates just haven't taken the required economics course that would enable them to understand why the fruits of their labor bring them two dollars a week while they're sold for three dollars a cup at Ishmael's.

Whatever you do, don't travel; don't meet people who are really different. You just might not be able to sleep comfortably after you do.

2. Don't move out of your gated community.

Gated communities afford real opportunities to exclude people whose economic status differs markedly from yours. Sometimes, these people will begin to wonder just exactly why their toilet-cleaning and bed-making pay seven dollars an hour while your investment banking pays over seven- hundred dollars and doesn't noticeably help anyone except those who occupy the top one percent of the tax rolls in the country.

Encounters with poor people in this setting are carefully controlled. Only maids, gardeners, and butlers, who are much too busy trying to feed their families to question you, are allowed past the security gates. The really poor but politically active, those who might actually join a union or even organize one, are kept safely at bay. Diversity is nice, but let's not get ridiculous about it.

3. Don't, under any circumstances, do volunteer work.

Most volunteerism puts you directly in contact with that most unpleasant group of the diverse—the have-nots. You'll think you're wonderful just because you're trying to help. In reality, often times all of your work will be met with the most uncomfortable question of all: "Is this the best you can do?"

§

Chapter 9:
The Myth of Philosophy

Philosophy is thought directed toward ultimate ends: the purpose of life, the essence of a human being, the price of that puppy in the window, the one with the waggly tail. Philosophers are those who sit around—or, better yet, lie around—drinking wine all day and engaging in profound cognition. In a sense, philosophers greatly resemble street people, except that the latter aren't able to apply for MacArthur Grants.

Although most of us are much too busy to think very much, we do have—deep within our culture—a grudging respect for people who possess the luxury and ability to ruminate. You can consider philosophers to be a little like your great-uncle Oliver. While you know that you couldn't stand to be around Oliver for more than a day at a time, you have to admit that he is quite entertaining at holidays. He can tell a couple of fun stories—usually the same ones he's told for the last thirty-seven years—and he can make a good bean dip. That's basically the way we look at philosophers. Except that their bean dips are pretty bad.

Although in the ancient world philosophers seemed to be hanging out everywhere—the market place, the Senate, and the brothel—today they make their homes almost exclusively in one of two places, the university or the think tank. Whereas philosophers in universities never consider whether their thoughts have any practical application, those who work in think tanks are always looking for ways to apply deep thought to the great and pressing problems of the world. And this is precisely where we start having difficulties. (For a list of old ideas retooled by think tanks, see *Table Ten*.)

Table Ten: Think Tanks in Our Lives: How Think Tanks Have Retooled Old Concepts

Old Concept	Rethought Concept
Blessed are the poor	Blessed are those removed from the welfare roles
The way that can be told is not the true way	The true way is the Flat Tax
Love your neighbor as Yourself	Mutually Assured Destruction
Buy American	Participate in the global economy
Honor your mother and father	Means-test your mother and father

Think-tankers would have us believe that thought is one of our most precious commodities and that those who think for a living are performing a public service. Is this really true? To find out, let's take a look at a young person just beginning her career of deep thinking.

Carrie Hoofsnagle is a junior at Gannon University in Erie, Pennsylvania. Maintaining a 3.95 GPA and working on a triple major in English, Philosophy, and Economics, she has long been her family's designated future attorney. But after watching C-Span one afternoon, her father becomes convinced that Carrie should eschew the law and instead pursue a path of glory by working for a conservative think tank. Since his epiphany, he has been having sent to her promotional material from the Cato Institute and the Heritage Foundation.

Carrie is somewhat resistant to the career guidance, but her father says, "Hey, honey, if you play your cards right, you could become the next Dinesh D'Souza or Alan Bloom or, even, god willing, Bill Bennett. Just think: 'My daughter, the drug czar.' It has a really nice ring."

Carrie says, "I don't know, Dad. It sounds weird to me."

During the early spring of her penultimate year of college, Carrie humors her father by applying for internships at a few think tanks. "You'll be a drug czar, yet," her father says to her each morning at breakfast.

Rejected by both Cato and Heritage, she's surprised to receive a letter of acceptance from the Right Thinking Institute, an up-and-coming ultra-right-wing think tank. Egged on by her father, she decides to accept the offer. On an early June morning, she hops on a Washington-bound bus. Arriving in our nation's capital at four in the afternoon, she takes the Metro to RTI so that she can meet the woman who has agreed to put her up for the summer.

After a twenty-minute subway ride and a short walk, she arrives at the red-brick building on the outskirts of Georgetown that houses the Right Thinking Institute. On the building's first floor is a Chinese Restaurant called "The Open Door Policy." She looks at the little gold plate on the door frame next to the entrance: "RTI: Thinking at its Rightest." Knowing that she's in the correct place, Carrie pushes a buzzer under the plate. After a few seconds, a young woman's voice comes through the speaker. "RTI, how can we help you?"

"Hi, I'm Carrie, the new intern. I'm looking for Nancy Updike, the woman I'm supposed to be rooming with this summer."

"That's me. I'll be right down to help you with your stuff."

Nancy buzzes the door open, comes down from the fourth floor, and takes Carrie up in the elevator to RTI's offices.

Next to the glass double doors for RTI is the entrance to a magazine marketed to expectant mothers. Nancy says, "Bill, that's our head thinker, doesn't regard pregnancy very highly. He thinks that its only function is to keep poor people so busy that they won't have time to form any sort of class consciousness. And it's okay for making our 'family values' clients happy too, but it's really messy. RTI thinks that children should be conceived in test tubes and raised in Skinner-like incubators. What do you think?"

A little tired from the long bus ride, all Carrie can manage to say is, "It sounds very Malthusian."

Nancy smiles and replies, "That's exactly the kind of thing-as-such that we need for our sound bites. It's vague, yet slightly intellectual. *Crossfire* will love it."

"We go on *Crossfire*?"

"Well, we don't, but Bill does, and when he says something while he's stroking his goatee, he looks really impressive. Part of what you'll do this summer is to help produce sound bites."

Carrie thinks to herself, *Dad will be so proud of me, writing Malthusian sound bites for a conservative think thank.* She asks Nancy, "Hey, does William Bennett ever come by here?"

"Why, he sure does; he's one of RTI's biggest underwriters. The trouble is that after every visit of his we have to air the place out because he likes to chain smoke while he pontificates about the drug problem. I'm sure you'll get a chance to meet him this summer. He's plugging his new book, *Beaten into Compliance: A Violent New Perspective on The Urban Education Crisis*."

"Wow," Carrie thinks, "I'm really in the big leagues now."

Nancy says, "We get all kinds of Right Thinkers here. Even Alan Bloom flew in from Chicago a couple of times. He and Bill used to quote passages from "The Apology" to each other while they ate peeled grapes and drank mulled wine. RTI finally had to ban him from the offices, though, because he kept trying to make out with all the male interns."

Since Carrie is tired, Nancy gives her a brief tour of the office and then takes her home. The two women make dinner and talk for a couple of hours. Then, wanting to be fresh for her first day of thinking, Carrie goes to bed.

At six-fifteen in the morning, Carrie is woken by the sound

of *Also Sprach Zarathustra* playing over the clock radio that Nancy has given her. Carrie climbs out of bed, goes to the kitchen, and starts the coffee maker. She hears Nancy singing to herself in the shower. Carrie is eating raisin bran when Nancy walks in to get some food. "It's all yours," Nancy says. "So today is your big first day. You meet with Bill at nine. You're going to be working with him. He requested you."

"Wow, the head thinker wants to work with me?"

Nancy smiles. "Yeah, he was very impressed with your background."

As Carrie showers, she realizes that she's becoming excited about her summer at RTI. She's actually going to be working for the head thinker himself. After finishing her shower, she goes back to the living room to put on a summer dress. Nancy comes in and says, "Hey, you don't need to wear that. Jeans and a t-shirt will be just fine. Bill says that we need to be comfortable when we think. If there's going to be a big-name guest, then Bill will warn us ahead of time, and we'll all put on good clothes. Otherwise, comfort is what we're after. You don't see Socrates wearing three-piece suits in 'The Apology.'"

"No, you don't," Carrie agrees. "But then again, he was drinking hemlock."

Nancy laughs. "You have a dark sense of humor. That's very good. Bill'll like that a great deal. You can use it when he hits on you later this summer."

"He hits on people? A thinker?"

"Certainly. Bill says that lasciviousness is one of the best types of thought. He's firmly convinced that John Rawls had fellatio in mind when he was writing *A Theory of Justice*. You know all that stuff about the veil of ignorance. Just what do you think was behind the veil?"

Carrie had never thought about it very much. Clearly, she realizes, she has a great deal to learn about thinking. The two women leave the apartment, get on the subway and head to Foggy Bottom.

When Nancy and Carrie arrive at RTI, they throw Carrie's bag into a cubicle. On the cubicle's inside walls hang old American World War II propaganda posters. One of the posters shows an American paratrooper drinking a Coke and dropping down into a field, probably somewhere in occupied France. The caption reads: "Your loose talk got there first."

Carrie looks at the poster and asks Nancy, "What's this all about?"

"Well, Bill feels pretty strongly that we need to be careful not to think aloud. Some of our thoughts are pretty heady and very important. Bill wouldn't want any of the competing think tanks or any of our philosophical enemies to get hold of what we're thinking of before it's ready."

"I see," Carrie says.

"Let me take you to Bill's office." The two women walk over to the door. Nancy knocks on the inside of the frame and says, "Hi, Bill. Carrie, your new intern, is here and ready to meet you."

Bill looks up from his desk and smiles. About forty years old and with jet-black hair that looks slightly greasy, Bill's wearing a black turtleneck. His skin's very pasty since he hasn't set foot in the sun in over seventeen years. Behind his desk is a framed sign that has a single word in red letters set against a blue background: "Think!"

Bill says, "Thanks, Nancy. Welcome, Ms. Hoofsnagle. So, you like to think, do you?"

Nancy walks back to her office.

"Come in and shut the door. We'll get to know each other."

"I'm so happy to be here, Mr. Michaels."

"Tell me a little bit about yourself."

Carrie begins to talk about her life in Erie, Pennsylvania. And Bill says, "Ah, yes, I remember your résumé now." He takes his glasses off, blows on the lenses, and then puts the spectacles back on his face. Carrie sees that when his glasses are off, his weak eyes, which he blinks incessantly, make Bill look like a newborn chick. He listens attentively, nodding every once in a while and saying, "Quite so, quite so."

After about twenty minutes of questioning Carrie and listening to her responses, Bill says, "Let me tell you a little about the project that we'll be working on together, Ms. Hoofsnagle. You've joined the RTI at a very auspicious moment in our history. We're working on a joint partnership with the private sector. I find thoughts punctuated by dollar signs to be very exciting. Don't you?"

Carrie had never really considered the idea before. But she supposes that thinking about money could be exciting.

Bill says, "It will be philosophy in service to mankind, especially its Swiss bank accounts. Don't you find that intriguing, Ms. Hoofsnagle?"

Seeing Carrie nod in agreement, Bill continues: "Our referral actually comes to us courtesy of Senator Steerforth, a Democrat from Mississippi. The Senator is an old friend of ours. One of my predecessors helped him to develop a philosophical underpinning for segregation."

Carrie's eyes widen. She had always considered segregation to be morally wrong.

Bill responds to Carrie's unvoiced concern: "Don't be so shocked, Ms. Hoofsnagle. Remember that the Right Thinking Institute deals in questions of practical or applied philosophy. Philosophy can be used to justify many things. Attila the Hun had his own philosopher. So did Hitler, and Franklin Roosevelt kept several in his Brain Trust. We may not always agree with our clients, but we must in every case provide them with the best possible cognition. Moreover, you will soon realize that there's something far more important than the actual philosophical quandary."

"What's that?"

"Billable hours, my dear. We must remember to generate as many billable hours as possible. The generation of revenue is what will help us to have our profession of thinking taken seriously. Just imagine what the state of philosophy would be like now if Confucius had billed at three-hundred bucks an hour."

"But," asks Carrie, "is what we do really worth three-hundred dollars an hour?"

"Ah, my dear, of course it isn't. But questions of exchange value have never stopped our professional brethren from making a bundle. So, why should they slow us down?"

Carrie's mind is beginning to reel. Her college philosophy teacher had never talked like this. Bill speaks with such vigor and enthusiasm that Carrie is literally borne aloft by the current of thinking.

Bill stops. He sighs and moves a paper clip around on his desk. "Well, I'm through day dreaming now. I see that you're a little discomfited by my diatribe. But one day, I assure you, if the Right Thinking Institute has anything to say about it, doctors of philosophy will be just as well-respected and remunerated as doctors of orthopedic surgery. But, in any event, where was I?"

"You were about to tell me about our new client."

"Yes, quite. Our referral, as I have said, comes from Senator Steerforth. The person in need of our philosophical help is one Mr. Joseph Legucci. Mr. Legucci is a real-estate developer from the state of Mississippi. He's fifty-seven years old...."

Carrie is taking notes on a legal pad that she has brought with her.

"And he's been building shopping malls for the last twenty-five years. These malls—thirty of them all over the country—have generated incredible amounts of money. They've provided countless thousands of teens with parking lots in which they can discover the fine art of necking. They're places in which the elderly can—without having to face the cold or those tacky street people—walk to their hearts' content in climate-controlled comfort. Mr. Legucci's malls have become places not only of commerce but of community."

Bill stops for a moment and repeats to himself: "'Commerce

and community,' that's a fine turn of phrase. Ms. Hoofsnagle, this is your first lesson in thinking. A philosophical argument may seem self-evident, but what it really needs, if it's going to be successful, is a good sound bite. Alliteration is often very helpful."

Carrie looks up from her pad and asks, "Okay, so his shopping malls have been a hit. What's the problem?"

"Well, Ms. Hoofsnagle, Mr. Legucci is reaching the age at which men begin to question the merits of their life's work. Senator Steerforth said, and I quote, 'Joe told me the other day that he thinks that maybe the malls were a bad idea. They're butt ugly, and they're all the same. They homogenize the culture, and they funnel people from the free public space of the downtown to the private space of the corporate corridor. They subvert democracy. It was the first time I ever heard old Joe use the word 'subvert.' I asked, 'Joe, are you becoming a Commie on me?' He said, 'Nah, I've just begun to think about things.' I knew right then that we were in trouble. 'Joe,' I said, 'you're not a thinker. Why don't we get some help with this?'"

Carrie says, "Well, most of Legucci's statements make sense. Malls are awful and—in the long run—bad for the country. What's the problem?"

"You're absolutely right, my dear. Malls are dreadful. But the problem lies in the fact that they generate a great deal of cash for certain people. And, in our case, what earned us the referral is that the Senator owns several-thousand acres of cheap real estate just east of Biloxi. And—until he began thinking—Legucci was going to build on this land a giant shopping mall, a palace of indoor commerce so gigantic that it would have its own subway system. The state of Mississippi stands to make perhaps as much as a billion dollars over the next ten years in tax revenue if the mall is actually built."

"And the Senator will probably make a bundle, too," Carrie says.

"You're starting to think, Ms. Hoofsnagle. I like the cut of your jib. And just consider all of the thousands of wonderful, low-wage service-sector jobs that will be created after the mall is built. But Mr. Legucci, in his autumn years, has found, much to the consternation of the Senator, both philosophy and literature. He has taken up the reading of William Faulkner novels.

"'I'm just a damned Snopes,' Mr. Legucci said to the good Senator. 'I'm trashing the land and creating a god-awful monument to greed and avarice that will last for decades.'

"'But think of the money, Joe,' the Senator had bleated.'

"'Senator, that's what I've been doing for the last twenty-five years, and look where it's gotten us. Entire downtowns have been turned into graveyards. A whole generation has grown up getting laid for the first time in the parking lots of American malls. It's not good. By god, Senator, all this is going to stop, with me at least.'

"The Senator came to me," Bill says, "practically in tears. His state needs that shopping mall."

"Why not just have another contractor build it?" Carrie asks.

"The trouble is—the Senator tells me—that Legucci's shopping malls tend to do very, very well. The state wants a good return on its investment. The Senator is so desperate that he's thought about kidnapping Legucci's grandchildren and sending severed limbs back to Legucci via Federal Express until he capitulates."

"All this over a shopping mall?"

"Well, it was over just a shopping mall until the RTI took the job. It's more than just a shopping mall now. It's a philosophical quandary. It's an epistemological question. It's teleology in the making. We have to build a case, one so overwhelming that Legucci can't help but want to build this shopping pantheon. He'll be compelled to. His very being will require it. He needs to see that it's good for the nation. And, you, Ms. Hoofsnagle, will be a special and important part of this ideological quest. You will aid me in convincing Mr.

Legucci—through flawless argumentation and free alcohol—that a shopping pantheon will be built. And after that, the Senator will send us a nice fat check for our consulting fees."

The RTI dedicates some of its best and most convoluted thought to the problem of getting Mr. Legucci to build the mall. Through extensive research and surveillance, RTI discovers that Legucci is a history buff, one deeply interested in the Civil War.

"Aha," says Bill, when Carrie presents him with a photograph showing Mr. Legucci grinning stupidly in the uniform of a Confederate Scout while standing in line at a McDonald's in Tennessee. "That is going to be our hook. We'll convince dear Mr. Legucci that this building project, let's call it the Mall of Northern Aggression, will help to memorialize the Civil War. I can see it now. There'll be a Japanese restaurant called "Gettysburg Genji," a new CVS pharmacy that we'll name "Appomattox Apothecary," and even "The Sound and Fury Stereo Shop."

Quickly getting into the spirit of things, Carrie suggests that the new movie house be called "Ford's Theater." Bill smiles when he hears the idea, and he says, "Wonderful, Ms. Hoofsnagle. I love the way you think. It's brilliant, absolutely brilliant."

The Mall of Northern Aggression would be a single three-story corridor running from North to South. Above the Southern entrance would be a giant ceramic bust of Jefferson Davis, and above the Northern entrance would sit an equally giant bust of Abraham Lincoln. All the mall employees would dress in blue or grey. But the glory of the Mall would be a real battlefield, located in the center of the complex. Each weekend the re-enactors would once again prosecute the War Between the States.

After the plan for the Mall of Northern Aggression is fleshed out in a briefing paper, Bill calls Senator Steerforth and asks him to bring Mr. Legucci to Washington for a lunch at the Georgetown Faculty Club. "I don't know, Bill," the

Senator says, "Joe doesn't really like coming to D.C."

"Well, Senator, tell him that Georgetown's school colors are blue and grey, to commemorate the valor of both sides in the War Between the States. And tell him that we can take him on a tour of Gettysburg if he wants."

"I don't know. What the hell does all of this have to do with building a god-damned mall?"

"Senator, just trust the Right Thinking Institute on this one. We've committed our best thought to the project. If you get Mr. Legucci here, we'll get your mall built."

"All right. It still sounds kind of weird to me, but my state needs this project. I'll see if I can get Joe to come up."

"Just remember to tell him about the Gettysburg tour, Senator."

Much to the surprise of Senator Steerforth, Joseph Legucci agrees to come to Washington. An elated Steerforth calls Bill to confirm that the two of them will be flying to the Capital. Bill smiles when the Senator tells him of the impending visit.

"I'm not surprised, Senator. All you have to do to get something accomplished is to commit a little thinking to the project."

The Senator says, "You think-tank boys are really something. I can't even get Legucci to meet me for drinks at the Oxford Inn. And I'm a fucking U.S. Senator. You just mention the Civil War, and Legucci is ready to jump on a plane."

"That's what you pay us through the nose for, Senator."

After a couple of weeks, the big day finally arrives. Bill had put Carrie in charge of preparations at the Georgetown Faculty Club. Blue-and-grey banners hang from the wall. One half of the waiters wear Union uniforms while the other half stand at attention in Confederate grey. Leaving no detail to chance, Carrie has even made sure that the day's special menu includes hardtack.

When the Senator and Mr. Legucci reach the club, Bill and Carrie greet them at the front door. Mr. Legucci is intrigued by the working model of a Confederate-issue twenty-pound cannon that Bill has had dragged from Arlington National Cemetery. As Mr. Legucci steps out of the limousine, Carrie touches the flame of a Bic lighter to the fuse. The cannon belches fire and smoke. The Senator, a survivor of Pork Chop Hill, instinctively shouts, "Incoming!" and dives for cover.

Mr. Legucci, though, whose wartime service had consisted solely of engaging in battles long-since fought, smiles and says, "Good God, it's a real Sartoris. The boys back home in the Twentieth Reenactment Battalion would love to have one of these."

Bill steps forward and grasps Mr. Legucci's hand. "On behalf of the Right Thinking Institute, welcome to the nation's capital." Shaking hands, Legucci is still transfixed by the cannon. Bill says, "Sir, I'm sure we can arrange to have this shipped to your battalion. Its presence will add yet another level of verisimilitude to your valuable living-history re-creations."

"Do you think we could find some grape shot for it?"

"I'm certain we can, Mr. Legucci."

While Bill and Legucci are talking, Carrie attends to the Senator—who, lost in the fog of battle— is trying to call in an air strike on a phantom Handy Talky. "Red One, this is Foxtrot," the shell-shocked Senator keeps repeating into his palm. Unfortunately, Red One never responds. He retired from the Air Force in 1957 and now owns twelve hot-dog stands in Daytona Beach.

Bill leads Mr. Legucci into the club, where the waiters salute the guests. Having regained his composure, the Senator is escorted by Carrie. The party sits down, and Bill introduces Mr. Legucci to the young thinker. "Sir, my able assistant, Ms. Carrie Hoofsnagle. She is the person responsible for the artillery salute that you received." Carrie holds out her hand, which, much to her surprise, Mr. Legucci tenderly kisses.

"What a wonderful treat, to find a young lady who is as historically aware as she is charming," Legucci says. Carrie blushes.

"Mr. Legucci," Bill says, "The RTI employs only the best young thinkers as interns."

They all begin drinking lemonade that has been prepared by women dressed in shawls and bonnets. Carrie is busily taking notes on two sheets of the handmade paper supplied at each place setting.

"My problem," Legucci says to Bill, "and I've told this to the Senator, is that I'm tired of shopping malls. I've built a heap of them, and, frankly, while they have made me a great deal of money, they're a real blot on the landscape. They leave me spiritually depressed. I'm tired of turning farmland into yet another Gap outlet. I went into architecture so that I could help people, so that I could make places and spaces that would give them a chance to be surrounded by beauty. After a while, the money just isn't important anymore."

Upon hearing the suggestion that money might not be important, the Senator becomes apoplectic and spews lemonade out of both nostrils. *God*, he thinks to himself. *If we still had the Committee on Un-American Activities, I'd bring this man up on charges*. Bill, urging caution, holds up his hand slightly and gives the Senator a napkin with which the lawmaker can wipe his nose.

Carrie had just read *Geography of Nowhere* and hadn't been very happy to be working on a project dedicated to screwing up yet more bucolic area. She had expressed this concern to Bill, who had said, "Miss Hoofsnagle, I sympathize with your position. But, don't you see, if you really think about it, how important this entire project is to the economy of Senator Steerforth's state? Moreover, careful thinking will elucidate the crucialness of this project to RTI. The good Senator is one of our most important—and wealthiest—clients. So, applying your powers of cognition to an objective analysis of the project's merits should help you to steer a course clear of your own prejudices. And, remember, your performance will be used in the evaluation process that determines whether you'll be invited back after graduation as a junior thinker. I believe that you have a bright future with RTI. I would encourage you not to endanger that future through weak reasoning."

Having seen which side her hardtack is buttered on, Carrie is dressed in the hoop skirt that Bill had borrowed from Ted Turner. She now nods in agreement with her boss, who's really working Legucci: "I think that perhaps some of your concerns vis-à-vis the environmental and esthetic impacts of helter-skelter building might be justified. But The Mall of Northern Aggression, unlike other shopping complexes, won't represent discontinuity with the past. Rather, a la Jane Jacobs, it'll suggest a radical conformity to its physical, historical, and intellectual surroundings."

"And there'll be working cannons, Joe," the Senator says, while wiping the lemonade off his suit.

"Working cannons, most malls just don't have those," Legucci says.

"They certainly don't," Bill adds. "Your mall, the Mall of Northern Aggression, will be an architectural wonder as well as an income and tax-generating center."

Leguci's opposition to the project begins to waver. Bill sees the look of indecision and says, "Mr Legucci, think about this. Can you conceive of a better way in which you can support the drive to promote history? Logically, you're the man who can do the living-history movement the most good. It would be a categorical abdication of your moral authority to do anything less. Don't you see that?"

Legucci bites into a piece of hardtack and chews slowly, as if meditating on the Civil War itself: "I can see it now," he says. "The rest-area gazebos will be named after the generals."

"Yes, of course, Mr. Legucci, although I recommend that we not use Stonewall Jackson. It might cause people to be uncomfortable."

"Excellent, excellent idea. All right, Bill, you and RTI have convinced me. I'll build the mall."

Letting out a whoop of joy, the Senator reaches for a flask that he keeps in his inside jacket pocket. He takes a short slug of whiskey and passes the flask around. The band that Carrie had hired begins to play a rendition of "When Johnny Comes Marching Home."

The Mall of Northern Aggression is built, and with money flowing into the leaky tax base of Mississippi and his own pockets, Senator Steerforth recommends the RTI to all of his colleagues. Carrie finishes out her summer at RTI and is indeed hired as a Junior Thinker two years later. After spending three years thinking for RTI, she is eventually hired by the Heritage Foundation, where she's now a senior thinker. She works on projects such as encouraging publishers to rewrite American history textbooks so that they show that George Wallace was one of the founding fathers and that Charles Darwin was a trouble-maker in the Kennedy Administration.

What not to do:

Thus, we can see what happens when people begin thinking. Things—usually fairly nasty ones—are accomplished. But there exist some concrete steps that you can not take to ensure that you think as little as possible.

1. Don't read.

It's a commonly known truth that most people who think a great deal have also read a great deal. If you simply must read, try to limit yourself to Curious George books. The Man with a Yellow Hat never really causes much damage. Don't, under any circumstances, try to read philosophy or literature. These kinds of reading materials abound with ideas. They're sure to get you into trouble. Try to pick books with lots of pictures, especially dirty ones.

2. Don't write.

Often, writing helps us to clarify our thoughts. Most thoughts, however, shouldn't be clarified. Rather, they should be discarded like sour milk. Not writing will help to keep your ideas bottled up tightly in your medulla oblongata, precisely the place in which they can do the least harm to the rest of the world.

3. Don't speak.

Talking to others is also a very important and useful way of clarifying our thoughts. If you speak, other people might actually agree with your harebrained ideas, some of which might be similar to their own mental drippings. If you must talk to others, make sure that you speak only about the weather or the price of a new Saturn. These are safe, neutral topics, ones that will keep you from causing any damage with wild plans and schemes.

§

Chapter 10:
The Myth of Social Activism

Does the following account sound familiar to you?

Last week eighteen zealots harassed law-abiding citizens, who were simply exercising their constitutional rights; the citizens were performing an act that—while objectionable—is quite legal. The zealots told the performers of the act that they—the law-abiding citizens—would go straight to Hell for continuing to perform it. Law-enforcement officials contacted about the harassment comment that they expect violence on the part of the zealots. Three days later, the newspapers deliver a report that the zealots actually have committed violence: there is a raid on a Federally-subsidized institution during which the zealots kill three workers.

A question to you, Dear Reader, who are these zealots? Do they sound like members of Operation Rescue in the process of vaporizing another abortion clinic? Well, they aren't. Actually, the above account is not of twentieth-century protesters of fetal destruction; rather, it details the exploits of the nineteenth-century abolitionist John Brown and his fellow rebels, who in 1859 mounted an attack against the Federal Arsenal at Harper's Ferry, Virginia. Along with Harriet Beecher Stowe, the raiders helped to trigger the American Civil War.

Although the ensuing conflict did in fact end slavery in the United States, it did so at a dreadful price. The South was turned into a smoking ash pile, and Yankee mercantilism, which was to bring us the sweatshop, McDonald's, and Chuck E. Cheese, triumphed across the nation.

But there's more to it than just that. The very people freed from slavery were for the next one-hundred years tortured and harassed by the war's losers. In fact, the only clear-cut victors in this conflict seem to have been the Yankee merchants and arms dealers who profited by providing supplies to the Union Army. The most educated and enlightened members of the Southern aristocracy, perhaps the very people most likely to have peacefully phased slavery out, were put six feet underground. The Southerners in charge during and after Reconstruction are the Rabble—those with no sense of vision other than one tinged by hatred. From these people, themselves bloodied by Yankee cavalry and bamboozled by Yankee Carpetbaggers, spring both the Ku Klux Klan and Jim Crow laws.

What's wrong with this picture? How could such putatively noble aspirations have led to a disaster, one entailing so much carnage and such misplaced use of energy? Reform attempts, especially those heralded by the loudest shouts and by the shrillest blasts on the trumpet, generally lead to the biggest tragedies. One has to break some eggs in order to make an omelette. Most of us, though, end up being eggs.

If the Civil War was disastrous to the moral fabric of the United States, then World War I was even worse in terms of what it did to the entire planet. The American entry into the Great War is a study in idealism gone astray. In 1917, the American Expeditionary Force, which is led by General Black Jack Pershing, steams overseas and proclaims to the French nation: "Lafayette, we are here." Lafayette has been dead for over ninety years. So, he's not impressed. Marshall Foch, though, the leader of the French Army, is more than happy to have some extra—and non-Francophone—bodies to replace his soldiers, who have been dying at an astonishing rate for the past three years.

The Americans arrive, get shot up for a year and a half, and then, just as boys from Georgia, Alabama, and Staten Island are learning to drink French wine instead of American rotgut, the Germans become tired of all the killing and are ready to revolt against their leaders. The Americans proclaim victory over war itself and then sail back to the New World. Subsequently, the French and English wave rubber chickens at the Germans, who become so pissed off during the next twenty years that they elect Adolph Hitler as their chancellor. All of the killing in the First World War, while designed to end armed conflict forever, merely serves to make the next war inevitable.

While American soldiers are busy trying to stop German imperialism, back on the home front, American women are busy attempting to stop American drinking. As the troops return in 1919, they find that their favorite bars have been closed down by the very people whom they had sailed off to protect.

Let's try to understand how the disaster of the First World War took place by looking at the life of one soldier who set out with Black Jack Pershing on the crusade to stop the Huns. In 1917, Walter Smith is a dirt farmer in Venango County, Pennsylvania. Like most Americans of his time and our own, Walter isn't really very concerned about saving Europeans from their own naughtiness. In fact, he might never have joined the other doughboys from Pennsylvania if he hadn't spent one Saturday morning in early June of 1917 at the Venango County Courthouse, listening to the war-mongering speech of Judge Jack Lovell.

Leader of the local Republican Party, the Judge was rumored once to have had lunch with President Woodrow Wilson. The Judge commented that the President was not such a bad fellow for an Ivy-League snob. Judge Lovell possesses a big belly growing ever larger from the beer he drinks before the leading local temperance meetings. Lovell had served briefly in the Spanish American War in a supply depot, although he claims that he has been a Rough Rider. Actually, he has never really ridden anything rougher than Mrs. Lovell. On this wonderful day in 1917, Judge Lovell is trying to recruit for military service many of the Pennsylvania farm boys who have come to town in order to sell their hogs.

Walter Smith arrives at the County Seat in the family wagon and in the company of his cousin Egbert. As they enter the town, the two young farmers hear a brass band playing

"Stars and Stripes Forever." Egbert asks his cousin, "What do you think that's all about?" Walter says that he doesn't know for sure but that it probably has something to do with the war. Egbert says that he doesn't understand why America would want to go to war against Germany, since he can't see what really awful thing that nation has done.

"Me, neither," replies Walter. "Let them English lords and ladies fight against the Huns if they're so bad. I just hope we can get through all the hoopla and sell our hogs. Then we can go and get us a couple of beers at the Pine Inn."

"Sounds good to me," Egbert says. The cousins bring their wagon into the town center and find themselves in the middle of a crowd standing near the courthouse. On a raised stand sits the Judge. Flanking him are two Marine officers resplendent in their brown uniforms and silver and gold insignia. After a while, the band stops playing. The Judge gets up and walks to a podium. He raises his hand, and the crowd of almost two thousand stops yelling and cheering.

"Friends," he begins. "Today is an auspicious moment in the history of Venango County. I'm going to offer no fewer than fifty of you the opportunity of a lifetime, a chance for glory, heroism, and, if you're truly fortunate, martyrdom. The two gentlemen on the podium with me are looking for half a hundred of the strapping young men in this fine town to leave behind their wives and girlfriends..."

"Or both!" a heckler from the audience shouts.

"...and travel" continues the Judge, after allowing a minute or two for the crowd to laugh, "with these gallant gentlemen on one of the most noble crusades that the world has ever seen."

Out of the audience of Pennsylvania farmers, many of whom have Mennonite and Amish roots, comes a question: "And just why, Judge Lovell, is this crusade so noble? What's so wonderful about killing Germans? They've never hurt us."

The Judge looks at his pocket watch. It's as if he's debating whether he has enough time to answer such an undignified question. After all, he has a beer blast scheduled for noon, followed by a prayer service at one and a temperance meeting at two-thirty. Then, he has another beer blast at three. Finally, after the second beer blast, he'll review the wording of a death sentence that he's going to deliver on Monday morning. He always makes these sentences as severe as possible. It's important, he feels, to keep the peasants in line.

The Judge points his fat finger at the heckler whose inquiry is so bothersome. He replies in a stentorian voice usually reserved for sentencing defendants to five years at hard labor: "Young man, I will answer your question. But to do so, I will have to dispute your assertion." The crowd doesn't consist of the most educated people in the world. Folks are therefore quite impressed with the Judge's use of the words "dispute" and "assertion." Judge Lovell continues: "My friends, it is wrong to say that the Hun has not hurt us. There is, of course, the sinking of the *Lusitania*, that ship bearing only innocent civilians, countless Americans among them." Eighty years later it'll turn out that the Lusitania was also carrying not quite so guiltless machine guns. The Judge continues: "Many Americans lost their lives in that sinking. But this certainly is not the single-most horrific atrocity perpetrated by the Huns." He stops for a moment and wipes his brow. Then he takes his handkerchief and blows his nose. This last action makes the Judge seem as if he is going to cry.

"Babies," he says, slowly and emphatically. The crowd is full of young, thick-bodied farm wives and their red-faced offspring. "Babies," he says again. "They impale babies on their damned spiked helmets." From beneath the podium, he produces a German helmet with a bullet hole through it, and he slams the helmet down on the top of the podium. "Excuse me, ladies, for my language. But one of our gallant French comrades-in-arms got the bastard..." Again he stops; again he wipes a tear from his eyes. Then he goes on: "Forgive my emotion, but we got the German scoundrel who did this..." Reaching beneath the podium again, he produces a stuffed doll and drives it down onto the spike of the helmet. A gasp goes up from the crowd, and, as if on cue, one of the cherry-faced children lets out a wail.

Walter looks at Egbert and says, “Well, that changes things in my mind. If the German V- boats...”

“U-boats,”—chimes in Egbert.

“V, U, Z, whatever, if the Huns want to blow up the *Lusitania*, that’s one thing. But when they start spiking babies, that’s something completely different; don’t you think?”

“I most certainly do,” says Egbert. “Why, just think what would happen if a mass of those Huns ever got in one of their Zeppelins and decided to float over the Atlantic and start spiking our babies. Hey, if they stopped in New Jersey or in Philadelphia, that might not be so bad. Some of those city babies could use a good spiking. But if they crossed the Schuylkill and come into God’s country, the heart of our nation, then that would be different. It could really threaten our entire way of life.”

Walter finishes his cousin’s thoughts: “Yeah, I just don’t cotton to having farm-fed babies spiked by German snobs. Just think, one minute, they’re listening to Beethoven, the next, they’re spiking a baby.”

“I don’t either,” agrees Egbert. “It could be your little sister, Irmagard, flopping around on that spike.”

Walter considers this image for a moment. And as he ponders the thought of his sister impaled on the spike of a German helmet, this generally passive farm boy becomes drunk with the passion of the patriotic: “By God,” he says to himself, “I’ve never hurt anyone in my life, but I really could kill those damn Huns, every single man Jack of them.”

While Walter is having the dream of the righteous, Judge Lovell is busy fanning the fires of hatred beginning to smolder in the normally gentle Pennsylvania farm folk: “As I said before, I will offer fifty of you strapping men the opportunity to go with the two honorable officers here.” He sweeps his arm back toward the two Marines in their tall hats. “You’ll have the opportunity to avenge the cruel murder of all those French and Belgian babies. You'll also have the chance to teach those treacherous Huns a lesson that they'll never forget, the lesson that the world won't stand for their bullying, that the good ol' US of A will fight for justice and against tyranny."

At the same time that the Judge is recruiting American cannon fodder, a French general on the Western Front is casually signing—between bites of his croissant— the order to shell a division of his own troops. After living in mud and filth for three years, the doomed soldiers have refused to fight on. These men have never seen any babies spiked by the soldiers in the pointy helmets. In fact, the German soldiers don't seem very different from their own fathers and brothers. The French High Command is terribly incensed that some of its troops would decide to throw in the towel prematurely. So it decides to blow them all up. After all, if troops decide to stop fighting on a regular basis, military careers will also flounder. People wouldn't be promoted, and factories wouldn't be pumping out flamethrowers and French Francs.

Back in Venango County, Judge Lovell has created quite a stir. The good farmers of Pennsylvania and their wives will not stand idly by and see innocent babies being killed. The Judge easily obtains for his two Marine friends the fifty recruits. These new soldiers practice their marching for the first time behind the brass band, which parades around the square. Among the recruits is Walter, who gives the hogs to his cousin Egbert for safe keeping.

Walter sees himself making Europe safe for the American way of life. He'll be a conquering hero who returns from Berlin at the head of a triumphant army. He's dizzy with dreams of glory. Meanwhile, the Judge comes around to each of the fifty volunteers and vigorously shakes hands. "My boy," he beams fifty times, "I really envy you. I only wish that the position of vast responsibility that I hold in the county didn't preclude the possibility of my joining you in the glory of combat."

When Walter is gladhanded by the Judge, Lovell looks

deeply into Smith's eyes and says, "Make us proud, my boy. Bring us back the head of a Hun, one of those baby-killer bastards."

Walter replies: "I promise I will, Judge, on my sister's honor. I'll make the world a really safe place again, a place where a man and his family can say and believe what they want."

Feeling the need for a strong drink before the Temperance Meeting that he's soon to chair, the Judge doesn't hear a word that Walter has said, but he mumbles that he's proud of Smith and his friends. The Judge wonders to himself how America's entry into the war will affect the stock market.

That afternoon Walter returns home and tells his Pennsylvania Dutch parents that he's going to go to Europe as a Marine and make the world safe for democracy.

His mother cries. His father is mostly apolitical, but he has some friends among the coal miners near Pittsburgh, and he has read a great deal of Eugene O'Neill. The elder Smith says, "Jesus Christ, Boy. Make the world safe for democracy? You're making the world safe for the munitions dealers. Did you sign anything?"

"Yeah, Pa, one of the Marine officers gave me a piece of paper to write my name on."

"Ah, Christ," the Father says, a look of despondency spreading across his face. "We have a little money this year. I'll get us a lawyer from Pittsburgh. We can take the enlistment papers to another judge and say that you were drunk or mentally unsound and didn't know what you were doing."

"Pa, I'm not mentally unsound. I knew what I was doing."

"Boy, if that old Temperance swindler talked you into going to Europe and shooting at a bunch of people who've never done you any harm, you are definitely unsound."

"But, Pa, I'm going to make the world safe for our little Irmagard. I don't want her to end up spiked on the end of one of those Hun helmets."

"Did Lovell throw some of that Limey propaganda at you? The Germans don't impale babies. Almost no one does. That's one of the oldest tricks in the world. Lovell told us that the Spanish were doing the same thing to Filipino babies back in ninety-eight, when some asshole blew up the *Maine*. I fell for it and ended up bayonetting a lot of people I probably would have liked. Why do you want to make the mistake I made?"

Walter's head swims with pictures of parades for conquering heroes. He says, "Pa, I don't know what you're talking about. Your country needed you and you went. I can't do any less."

"You have to make your own decisions. If you want to go, go. See for yourself. If you're still alive at the end, come back. The farm will still be here for you, and we'll go get a drink together." Two days later, Walter marches off from the town square to the train station with forty-nine other savers of the world. The train speeds Walter and his comrades off to Camp Xenophobia, where they are prepared for their trip overseas and the combat that will follow.

Fast forward to early September of 1918. Walter is sitting in the mud and filth of the American sector of the Western Front. Shells whistle over his head. And the staccato chatter from the machine guns echoes across No-Man's Land. Of the fifty boys from Venango who marched away the summer of 1917, thirty-two are dead. Ten were killed when a shell from a German Big Bertha landed neatly on the company headquarters tent. Another fifteen died when part of the earthen wall shielding them from the Germans collapsed. The fifteen, three of whom were in the process of relieving themselves, exposed themselves to the accuracy of a former piano player from Manheim. The virtuoso that he was, he rapped out a deadly tune on a water-cooled machine gun. Four others were shot through the head by snipers. And three simply disappeared into the ooze of No-Man's Land during a raid into the German trenches.

Of the eighteen who are still alive, nine lie wounded in the hospital. The remaining nine have never once seen an impaled French baby. They have, however, witnessed several French and English firing squads summarily dispatching private soldiers who thought that the orders of the Allied High Command were objectionable. These nine remaining heroes from Venango County are lousy, tired, and frightened.

Walter Smith has found himself wishing that he had availed himself of the services of the lawyer that his father had recommended. Despite his misgivings about the joys of military life, Walter is the only one among the surviving nine soldiers from Venango County to become a true hero. He received a bronze star for the dubious honor of killing eight Germans in a machine gun nest with a hand grenade. After he had tossed the grenade and shot the two soldiers who had tried to escape from the nest, Walter inspected the Hun layer and found absolutely no trace of dead babies, only a few photographs of some live ones and their mothers. Both the babies and their mothers bore a strong resemblance to their Pennsylvania Dutch counterparts.

Walter has, as far as he knows, liberated no one and nothing. Everything seems to be completely out of whack. He feels angry and despondent. If Walter had only employed the technique of Locus of Control, life would have been much better. This technique helps its practitioners to recognize that they create the conditions in which they find themselves. People are responsible for their own lives. If Walter had employed this technique, he would have realized that he created the mud and the filth in which he lived. He created the bullets overhead. He created the munitions dealers and other plutocrats who profited from the war. He created it all. Unfortunately for Walter, the technique of Locus of Control isn't to be pioneered until 1974. So, Walter just remains pissed off. (See *Table Eleven* for ways in which Walter could have employed the Locus of Control Technique.)

Table Eleven: Locus of Control Technique

Event in Walter's Life	Event Mediated by Application of Locus of Control Technique	Walter's Unmediated Reaction
Bullet hole in leg	"This is an excellent opportunity for practicing breathing exercises."	"This hurts like a mother fucker."
Best friend eviscerated	"I can process my grief and express it in socially acceptable ways."	"Let's shoot the officers."
Cockroaches in food	"Where there are lemons, I can make lemonade."	"Yech."
Guy in pointy helmet trying to stab him.	"Maybe we can work to meet our mutual needs."	"Where's my fucking pistol?"
Entire First World War	"I can't control others. I can only control my reactions to them."	"Let's shoot the officers."

Mail from home tells him that Judge Lovell's stocks have done so well that the Judge has built a brand new home with the annual dividend. Ma is very happy that Walter has so far survived fairly unscathed. She says that the Judge has made a point of visiting every home with a young man overseas. And she just doesn't understand why Pa had met the Judge with a shotgun when he visited their farm. Pa writes that his armed encounter had been one of the high points of his—Pa's—life. The elder Smith argues that if people had received the Judge with shotguns back in the summer of 1917, maybe the Jackson boys wouldn't have been blown up.

Buoyed by the correspondence from home, Walter observes the armistice in November with a mixture of relief and mourning. He is glad to be alive, but the world is now full of angry Communists and really dispirited Germans. Things don't seem to be much safer than they were when he marched off eighteen months earlier.

In May of 1919, Walter and three other survivors from Venango County—the rest had either died in the hospital or disappeared into France—sail into New York Harbor. Walter then takes a train to Pittsburgh, where his father meets him. "I don't suppose we can have that beer now?" Walter asks.

"You know that Prohibition was passed just before you came home," his father lugubriously replies. "Lovell was ecstatic. He said that it would help to provide a wholesome environment for the returning heroes—all goddamn four of them. Rumor has it that Lovell partnered up with some guy from Boston—Kennedy, I think the name is—and is making a fortune running booze down through Erie. I'll be damned. A man goes off to war and can't even come home and get a decent drink. The country's going straight to hell."

These are the results of the War to End all Wars: riots in Germany, revolution in Russia, and closed bars in America. Prohibition itself would in turn create the FBI and subject Americans to wiretaps and the not very flattering house dresses worn by J. Edgar Hoover.

What not to do:

Most attempts to change the world end in disaster. When people ask you to embark upon an adventure that promises to make the world a better place, you should do your part for humanity by running away screaming.

Here are some concrete things that you can not do to help avoid disasters such as the one that embroiled Walter. (For a short list of disasters caused by Social Activism, see *Table Twelve*.)

Table Twelve: A Brief Tour of Disasters Caused by Social Activism

Social Activist	Action	Disaster Caused by Action
John Brown	Raid on Harper's Ferry Arsenal	Civil War
Vladimir Lenin	Creation of Workers' Paradise	Russian Revolution, purges
Carrie Nation	Smashing up bars	Prohibition, rise of organized crime
John Steinbeck	Writing about plight of dust-bowl Okies	Snubbing by Sinclair Lewis
George Orwell	Writing *1984*	Perpetuation of 40-year Cold War
Alvin Toffler	Description of Future Shock	Rise of Newt Gingrich
Producers of "We Are The World"	Video encouraging understanding and respect	Further enriching of Michael Jackson

1. Don't go to large public meetings.

People will do odd things—such as beating each other up, thinking that Jacob Purdey is wise, or marching off to certain doom—that they would never dream of doing by themselves or with just a small group of friends surrounding them. Peer pressure is notorious. You didn't have that first drag off a cigarette by yourself, did you? You weren't brave—or stupid—enough to do dumb things on your own. No, you needed to be goaded into doing them by people even more gelatinous than you are. What goes for smoking or drinking goes doubly for joining a reform movement or agreeing to march off to Iraq in search of Saddam's head. So, next time you hear about a public meeting called to discuss a burning issue, do us all a favor and stay home.

2. Don't be swayed by stories of people being brutalized.

There are two reasons to not be snookered by these stories. First, and most important, much of the time these stories aren't true. As Walter learned, there were no impaled French babies. Yet, and perversely, through participating in the war Walter helped to assure that there would be people taking gas showers in the 1940s. When people tell you that you should help poor unfortunates in some remote corner of the world, you'll often find that these very same people are not coming with you when you set out on your mission of mercy. They can be of more service to the cause—so they tell you—from home.

Second, when these stories do occasionally turn out to be true, rest assured that your country is not acting out of the goodness of its own heart by interceding in the affairs of some distant nation. For example, Roosevelt knew all too well about the German death camps, but he didn't do anything to blow them up. Contrary to popular myths, America didn't wage war against the Germans to save the inmates of Auschwitz; rather, the U.S. fought the Huns a second time in order to secure American hegemony in Western Europe and to prevent the eventuality of English and American babies being christened with names like Vladimir and Serge. Be suspicious of all good intentions, especially when they're writ on such a huge scale.

3. Don't start reading about distant places.

Ignorance, in some cases, really is bliss. The more interested you are in the terrible state of affairs in some distant (or even not so distant) part of the world, the more likely it is that you will want to help. And by helping, you're very likely to make things worse, not better. Do us all a favor and just finish your own work. Don't pay attention to your neighbors. If the screaming from next door becomes too loud, just close the windows and lower the blinds. §

Chapter 11:
The Myth of Vision

We're almost at the end of our tour through the realm of self-esteem. But no journey through these outlands would be complete without going back in time to where it all started, to the very first instance of someone—jerk that he was—saying, "Aha!" From this primordial ejaculation were born the first vision statement, the first flip-chart, and the first pie graph. Humanity has been going downhill ever since. So, in the words of Sherwood Schwartz, "Sit right back, and you'll hear a tale."

Welcome to the dawn of time. Each morning our prehistoric ancestors arose, ate, shagged, defecated, scratched a little, and were sometimes chased by big hairy things that went bump. Then one fateful day, one of these ancestors of ours—Oog—scratched and said to Boog, his live-in cave-mate of indeterminate gender, "You know, I'm just not satisfied anymore. Maybe there's something better."

Boog was quite proficient at running from big hairy things, but he lacked any sort of vision. He replied: "Well, we're doing what we've always done. Why don't you defecate a little and shag me? You'll feel better afterwards."

Oog was not having any of it. "I'm still not satisfied. We could do better than this. I have a dream of how things could be. Boog, you and I could go into business for ourselves. We could move out of this cave and into a split-level hovel."

"What could we do?" asked Boog.

"Well, I'm not sure," replied Oog. "I don't know exactly what kind of business we could have. But, I'd be the idea person, and you could be the manager."

"I just have one question," said Boog.

"What is it?" replied Oog.

"What's an idea?"

There's the root of the problem—theirs and ours: an idea,

dissatisfaction, ambition. Up until Oog decided to rock the boat, everything was going just swimmingly. But it was that one moment when Oog wanted to be something else, something better, wanted to break the birth/death cycle, to square the karmic wheel, that he really began to cause trouble. Oog posited his existence against the meaninglessness of the universe and started the whole trend of making everything really uncomfortable for the rest of us.

Six months after his conversation with Boog, Oog was developing a vision statement and a plan for the first prehistoric service industry, a mastodon extermination company called Oog and Boog, Inc. At first, Boog, the manager, had a difficult time. He could never keep any employees, since they were without fail eaten or crushed. They would simply run up to the big furry things and throw a couple of small rocks. Annoyed by these creatures, the mastodons promptly dispatched the offending employees.

Boog, besides being the human resources manager, also did the numbers. One day he went to Oog in a very gloomy mood and said, "Look, we aren't doing too well. None of our customers will pay us, because we haven't exterminated even one mastodon. And our employee retention rate is atrocious. The ones who aren't killed just want to shag, defecate, and scratch all day. If this keeps up, we'll be out of business really soon. You're the one who's supposed to come up with ideas, whatever they are. So, why don't you have one?"

Oog could have replied, "Oh, the hell with it. Let's just scratch, eat, defecate, and shag some, like we've always been doing." But he decided to buck nature, to take a stand against irrationality. And the course of humanity has been changed for the worse ever since. He would have an idea. He wasn't quite sure how to have one. But he would, for the good of Oog and Boog, Inc.

Oog went for a walk and began to think. At first, all he developed was a rather severe headache. Eventually, though, an idea began to emerge. Slowly at first, but then gradually faster, the idea arrived: It didn't make sense for his employees just to run helter-skelter up to a mastodon and fling stones at it. They had to do something else.

After scanning his memory for an incident in which a mastodon had been killed, Oog remembered a time when he had been chased by a mastodon into a narrow gulch. Because the monster had been closing in on him and because of the narrowness of the gulch's walls, there had been nowhere for Oog to run, and he had thought he was a goner. His legs gave out, and he realized that he would probably never shag Boog again. But then something really strange happened. The earth began to shake. A giant boulder at the top of the canyon vibrated and then fell right on top of the mastodon, completely crushing it.

As Oog's headache subsided and he thought about the experience, his synapses began to fire: "Let's see," the world's first idea man said to himself: "The mastodon was alive when it chased me into the gully. And then a big rock fell on it." Finding "Aha!" for the very first time in the soon-to-be-sordid history of humanity, Oog proclaimed to himself: "I understand. Whenever a mastodon chases a person into a gully, the earth will shake and a big rock'll fall and kill it. So, all we have to do is have one of our employees run into the gully, and the earth will shake, and a big boulder'll fall on the mastodon and kill it. It's rational, and it's simple." (For a brief listing of famous "Aha!" moments, see *Table Thirteen.*)

Table Thirteen: Ten Famous "Aha!" Moments

Person who said "Aha!"	**Sentence following utterance of "Aha!"**
Christopher Columbus	"I bet those guys would love to work in copper mines."
Satan	"She'd love an apple."
Kevin Costner	"I bet I'd be even better as a director."
Builder of the Hindenburg	"Hydrogen has twice the lifting power of helium."
Henry Ford	"Wouldn't an assembly line be a boon to industrial workers?"
John F. Kennedy	"The Bay of Pigs is a great place to teach the Commies a lesson."
Lyndon Johnson	"So is Vietnam."
Ronald Reagan (after onset of Alzheimer's)	"So is Cleveland."
Regis Philbin	"Greed would be a great basis for a game show."
William Jefferson Clinton	"Hey, those interns sure are cute. No one will ever have to know."

Electrified by his idea, Oog raced back to the cave where Boog was busy scratching.

"Boog, I have an idea. By George, Boog, I think I've really got it." He then frantically explained his notion to his cavemate, who nodded a great deal while scratching.

"Well, Boog, what do you think?" Oog asked when he had completed his diatribe.

Boog said, "It sounds great. I just have one question."

"What is it?"

"Who's George?"

The next day, Oog assembled his remaining employees and announced his plan, sketching it out on a flip chart. Oog asked for a volunteer to lead the mastodon into the gully. One of his employees suggested that since it was Oog's idea, he should be the one to execute it. Oog told the employee that while the suggestion was greatly appreciated, he—Oog—shouldn't be the one to carry out the operation since he was the idea man. His talents were much too valuable to be risked in such a fashion. Thus was born the division of labor that we have today: some nitwit with money develops a ridiculous idea and expects someone else to bear the consequences of carrying it out. After promising to double the share of mastodon meat that would be distributed, Oog found an employee—Retch—who wasn't very bright but who was willing to lead the creature into the gully.

Anticipating by about four million years the First Battle of Bull Run, the big day arrived. All of the staff of Oog and Boog, Inc. gathered at the top of the gully. Retch went out into a field and threw a stone at a very big and quite hairy mastodon that was quietly minding its own business. Irked by the little shit who had the temerity to bother it, the mastodon began to chase Retch, who led it into the gully, where Oog and the rest of the employees stood in their loin cloths by the flip chart.

Screaming in terror at the top of his lungs, Retch streaked into the gully about twenty feet in front of the mastodon. The assembled observers waited in anticipation of the coming technological triumph. Oog told them not to worry. Everything would be fine, since rocks would automatically drop into the gully. The boulders, though, oblivious of their preassigned role in Oog's scheme, did not hurl themselves down from upon high. The mastodon quickly closed the gap between itself and the unfortunate Retch, who was trampled beneath one of the creature's big feet.

All the onlookers were, of course, disappointed. The value of shares of Oog and Boog, Inc. dropped ten points on the NASDAQ. Undaunted by the sudden reversal of fortunes, Oog immediately called for another volunteer. The plan had been flawless. Obviously Retch had done something wrong. Perhaps he had not flailed his arms in the manner that would induce the rocks to fall. All that was needed was a better worker, certainly not a better plan. In order to secure the requisite guinea pig, Oog generously offered to quadruple the amount of compensation that the successful employee would receive. And in keeping with the maxim that every outrageous plan usually finds an idiot hungry and desperate enough to see it through to disastrous fruition, another volunteer did in fact step forward. In this case, it was a rather hirsute creature named Rolf.

Meanwhile, the doubting Boog was trying to talk Oog out of the new scheme: "Look, why don't we just forget the whole thing and go back to scratching and shagging. Things weren't too bad then. Besides, we're really starting to run out of employees now."

Oog shot back that the lives of a few workers were nothing in comparison to the great stride forward that the company—and humanity itself—would make when the boulders—as Oog knew that they must—crushed the mastodon. Boog said that it was easy for Oog to talk like this when he wasn't the one being chased. Oog was practically crying tears of frustration because of the stupid incomprehension of others. He responded that Boog just didn't understand how these things worked, that Oog possessed the one commodity that Boog and the rest of the employees would probably never have: vision. Boog said that he didn't understand what vision was, but he did understand that they were quickly running out of employees. And he sat down against one of the boulders to await the coming debacle. (See *Table Fourteen* for seven visions that should have been impaired.)

Table Fourteen: Seven Visions That Should Have Been Impaired

Napalm
Eight-track tapes
Levittown
Breast Implants
Telemarketing
Non-refundable bottles
Sports-Utility Vehicles

While Oog and Boog were discussing the shortcomings of the plan, Rolf had attracted the attention of yet another mastodon. And by the time Boog had sat down against the rock, the mastodon, an ancestor of the elephant that would dance on the chest of Fred Blivens, was having a great deal of fun chasing Rolf. The Cro-Magnon person was screaming in a manner that Oog now considered quite inappropriate for an employee of the company. He made a mental note to write a new rule in the employee handbook prohibiting shrieking.

The mastodon entered the gully just one or two large steps behind poor Rolf, whose prehistoric life flashed in front of his eyes. Boog felt something crawl down his neck. He leaned back hard against the boulder in order to kill his visitor. The boulder rolled into the gully. As blind luck would have it, the mastodon was almost directly parallel to the scratching Boog and the cascading boulder. Thus, the faithful Rolf survived to shag another day.

Oog proclaimed his plan an incredible success. The said success was, of course, due to Oog's foresight in the choice of Rolf, who had gesticulated in just the proper manner. Boog was feeling much better after scratching his back against the boulder. He suspected that another mechanism was at work. But he could not precisely articulate what it was.

After the crushing of the mastodon, the success of Oog and Boog, Inc. was assured. Neanderthals and Cro-Magnon people from as far away as Cleveland Heights began to bid for Oog's services It did take, however, the death of another fifty-two employees and eight more itchy backs on the part of Boog for Oog to clearly determine what had caused the boulders to fall into the gully.

What not to do:

What the exploits of Oog and Boog, Inc. demonstrate is that any idea—no matter how stupid—can be carried to fruition if only there exists a pool of people desperate and unaware enough to execute it.

As you might have guessed by this point, there are some steps that you can take in order to assure yourself—and the rest of us—that your vision, whatever it may be, will come to nought. If only Oog and Boog had heeded the following advice, we might have been spared the disaster of untold numbers of vision statements, marketing plans, and "Aha!" moments.

1. Don't ever say "Aha!"

Also, eschew "Eureka," "Gadzooks!" "Excelsior," "I've got it!" and, "Fucking Ay!" All of these expressions clue in your friends to the fact that you've had an idea. One of your buddies—looking for something to do after work—just might listen to you. Worse, that friend might agree with your idea. And, worst of all, that friend might even help you to make your idea reality. Then we're all in deep do-do. Do you have a good idea? Shut up.

2. Avoid developing your vision.

You can't tell people your ideas if you don't have any

in the first place. Don't think about the way you'd like the world to be in one-hundred years, twenty years, five years, one year, or even the day after tomorrow. The planet will be just fine without your new subdivision, consulting company, or overpriced organic grocery store. The only kind of vision you should work to develop is tunnel vision. Just keep walking, buddy! Easy does it!

3. Don't look for new ways of doing the same old thing.

If it's not broken, don't fix it. Innovation is not all it's cracked up to be. If you look closely at the vision statement of any entrepreneur, you'll see the palimpsest of "Bad Ideas Past." Right behind all those new subdivisions, lurks the Enclosure Movement, the gutting of inner cities, and *Chia Pets*. We need many things in this world. But a new sense of vision is definitely not one of them.

§

Chapter 12:
The Myth of Sisyphus

Congratulations: you've arrived at the end of the book, but certainly not at the end of the insanity caused by people with very high self-esteem. Let's briefly retrace our path through the outlands of desire. We've toured the educational system that allows people like Iggy to terrify people like Winston. Through witnessing the shenanigans of our textbook representative, Tiffany, we've seen the pernicious effects of planning. We've pulled back the flap of the sweat lodge and watched as Lisa Jones at Ishmael's Caffeine Machine developed a marketing vision that will leave most of us with shaky hands and the rest of us with slashed paychecks. Through looking over the shoulder of budding young screenwriter Fred Zalston, we've seen the dreck that passes for creativity these days. And by following around J.B. Downing, we've learned that those who espouse diversity usually speak with a forked tongue. Can philosophy and self-actualization help us out of our quandary? No, the adventures of Carrie Hoofsnagle at the Right Thinking Institute and Michael Ginley at the Formula have shown us that those routes are pretty much dead-ends.

But if the present is depressing, we've seen that the past is just as icky. By returning to the thrilling days of yesteryear, we've seen that the roots of self-esteem run very deep. Because of a strong commitment to social action, the doughboy Walter Smith helped to set the stage for World War II, the Cold War, the Korean Conflict, the Vietnam War, and probably that nasty fight you had last week with your cousin Elizabeth. Our intrepid pickpocket, Brother Raoul, looked deep within himself and found the strength that allowed him to get several-thousand people butchered in a meaningless religious war. Our favorite vampire, Vlad Dracul, also looked inward and found the courage to become a violent and pathological control freak, thus securing matching IMF grant money for the people of fifteenth-century Wallachia. And last, but certainly not least, we've learned—through the primordial experience of Rolf and Retch—that when someone says, "Aha!" our response should be, "Oh oh."

So, where do we go from here? Nowhere. What do we do? Nothing? With whom should we consult? Nobody. Let this volume of stories act as your Circumlocution Office, as your Categorical Imperative. Sit in your room, pull down the blinds, and breathe deeply. You won't accomplish very much, but, hey, that's just fine.

I will close this volume of cautionary tales with a *Table of Mayhem* that you can refer to in the coming days, months, and years. Whenever you have a profound thought, immediately review the table, mix yourself a strong drink, and take a nap. When you awaken, you'll probably have no memory of whatever diabolical scheme initially came to your mind. And the rest of us will be saved from the misery of having to perpetually roll our stones up the corporate, religious, or philosophical ramp.

I bid you adieu and wish you no luck at all.

§

Table of Mayhem

Character	Occupation	Dream	Resulting Mayhem
OOG	Paleolithic entrepreneur and idea man	Mastodon Extermination Company	Corpses
BROTHER RAOUL	Medieval pickpocket	A Successful Crusade	More Corpses
VLAD THE CARESSER	Heir to Wallachian throne and future vampire	A kinder, gentler Wallachia	Quiche Lorraine and even more corpses
WALTER SMITH	World War I doughboy	A world safe for democracy	Prohibition
WINSTON NEBBISH	Ninth grader	A good education	Torn underwear
LISA JONES	Marketing guru	*Tashtego Tanzanian*	Ten-million highly literate caffeine buzzes
CARRIE HOOFSNAGLE	Intern at right-wing think tank	The Mall of Northern Aggression	Twelve more Gap outlets
FRED ZALSTON	Budding screen writer	"Saving Private Ryan's Credit Rating"	A coke and a smile
TIFFANY JOHNSON	Textbook company sales rep	High sales of *To Market, To Market*	Mass Illiteracy and student apathy.
MICHAEL GINLEY	Stoner	Getting it	A career as an expert medical witness
J. B. DOWNING	Publisher	Worktopia	Falling profits and land mines in the lobby.

About the Author:

Although hundreds of respectable editors and pubishers probably wonder how the admissions process could have gone so horribly wrong, Douglas W. Texter is a graduate of a highly esteemed publishing course and has developmentally edited a number of best-selling college textbooks. Texter has also taught Literature, Composition, and Publishing Industry courses at several colleges that certainly want their names withheld. Texter also edits dissertations and writes fun-filled content for rhetoric-textbook websites.

Texter's humor has appeared in *The Door* and the *Amityville House of Pancakes*. His first short story, "A Dangerous Day," was published in The Urban Bizarre in September 2003. Having also edited medical journals, proofread discovery-deposition transcripts, and canvassed for Greenpeace, Texter will be finishing a Ph.D. in English at a university that probably wonders why it ever let him in. Texter's hobbies include collecting lint, checking e-mail, and making truly terrible coffee.

§

www.ingramcontent.com/pod-product-compliance
Lightning Source LLC
LaVergne TN
LVHW011347080426
835511LV00005B/169
* 9 7 8 1 8 9 4 9 5 3 2 0 7 *